God
Given

Answers To Your Questions

Volume I

Enlightened Path Publishing
Post Office Box 5081
Huntington Beach, CA 92615

A portion of the sales goes toward education and various projects to help instill compassion. The goal is to bring peace… to end suffering and make joyful the lives of all inhabitants of this planet earth. Know that change is coming for it has already begun.

Please note: The information in this book is not intended to replace medical or veterinary care.

Cover photograph courtesy of Getty Images
ISBN: 978-0-692-87998-6
Contact: Enlightened Path Publishing
www.AngelsandIntuition.org

Printed in USA

Editor's Appreciation

To my Angel Guides... thank you for your gentle encouragement and unending patience. Your beautiful words lift me and bring peace.

To my dear Brother, Yeshua... you are a part of me. Everything I am and hope to be is rooted in your essence.

To my dad... for your unwavering support and exceptional spiritual teaching. Our friendship means so much to me.

To my mother... for introducing me to ACIM. Your kindness sets you apart from anyone I've ever known.

To David, Bob, Angelica, Jen, family and friends... thank you for your love and support. You've taught me about faith, loyalty, hope, and perseverance.

Photograph by LotusFlowerMeaning.com

Table of Contents

Saint Francis of Assisi statue

The Incredible Beauty and Wonder
Breathed Into Each Human Life
Is Worth the Pain Endured…
For No Pearl Forms
Without the Irritating Grain of Sand.

We have compiled various subject matter and answered some of your questions to help you on your journey. This manual is intended to be studied over a period of several weeks or perhaps months. Do not rush through it, Dear Ones, as you do everything else in your harried lives. Refer to it often.

There are few requirements. You need only to pay attention… and skip no homework. This will not be a graded assignment. Nor is it pass or fail. Truly it is impossible for you to fail. Once you complete the work, you will have passed with flying colors.

If you have followed our instruction, you will begin to look at your world through different eyes. Where once you felt the pull to join in a game of rough and tumble, you are likely to sit one out, preferring to enjoy basking in the sun or playing with your children. You will think you are lazy or coming down with the flu. And some of you will acquiesce to the pressure from your peers. But the seeds have been planted. Change is coming and you are ready for it.

So once again we remind you to pay attention. Be aware of your surroundings and the subtle breezes as they stir up the stagnant, transforming it into flow and movement. That will be your first clue that you are beginning to awaken from your slumber. Embrace it.

That is all we need say, Dear Ones. Begin your reading and call on us whenever there is need.~

Chapter 1:
Relationships

*O*ur discussion on relationships begins with an explanation. There is much confusion as to its general purpose. Let us offer clarity to better understand this. All souls are searching for what they perceive to be the missing pieces of their being. In truth, there are no missing pieces. Nevertheless, that is the perception. It has been set in motion and cannot be rescinded on a whim. So the highly inquisitive human mind endeavors to collect its misplaced fragments by joining with other souls.

There is something to be gained from every encounter. It is the classroom, and you are both student and teacher. Chronological age of the form [body] has no relevance. Your roles are continually changing within the lifetime and from one incarnation [life] to the next. Completing the assignment [life lesson], you close a chapter and turn the page. Classmates change… instructors come and go. It is all divinely orchestrated to bring you to the next phase of your soul's development. If the Children of God [you] only knew this, you would approach relationships in a radically different way.

Humans see relationships as unique in scope and application, but truly, they are all the same. It is Love's expression reflecting back to you. Your connection to like-minded souls, as you see it, is proof of your existence. It is your attempt to define the Self. You do not know who you are, so this is the process you use to answer the question. This is part and parcel of human thinking and a window into the workings of the human mind.

You believe relationships are for companionship, procreation, and accumulation of monetary wealth. These are mere byproducts. It is secondary focus, and oftentimes, distraction. You endeavor to find those souls who will agree with you… those with whom you can "bounce" ideas off of and share your innermost thoughts and feelings. What you are really seeking is validation.

We will demonstrate… The customer or supervisor assigns you tasks, confirming your value and sense of purpose. The mate, giving you his attention, is proof that you are lovable. Your children come to you for advice or comfort, and so you feel needed. The offspring are further proof that you walked the earth and made your mark.

But what about the friction and dissention in those very same relationships? The moment you disagree, a line is drawn in the sand. You each take your prospective sides. Winning becomes the prize you must have at all cost. You stare with contempt at your once beloved study partner, now adversary and nemesis. But you are misreading all you see. Why do you equate empty victory and defeat of a brother [masculine pronouns are used throughout the book – see p. 149] with your value and deservedness? If you lose, do you cease to be worthy of love? Apparently this is your belief… and the ego is ready to fight to protect the illusion it has procured.

The faulty belief system wreaks havoc and is the source of tremendous pain. You marry just to find the flaw in your spousal choice, and so manage to dissolve the union soon after. The child you adored grows to adulthood, and you are filled with pride. But on the day he was born, you laid upon his tiny shoulders your wish for perfection of Self. The offspring standing before you is a mirror. And the mirror reflects back all aspects of your humanness… not just those you deem admirable. So the image of perfection could not be sustained. Flawed and imperfect, you condemn what you made because he shattered the illusion you held so dear.

It should be apparent by now that your inclination to silence, to kill the disagreeable features within relationships, is a futile and deadly objective. It can only lead to harm in the name of self- (ego) preservation. Alas it has been revealed! Nothing stands in the way of solving the problem of relationships. Moving forward, without the burden of fighting for position and false justice, we can approach relationships simply, head on.

First, know that every relationship is Holy. Yes, we said *every* relationship. It is precious because all beings –

everyone you meet — are aspects of self. Hence, denial of a brother is denial of self. For every rejection of God's creation, there is pain and self-condemnation tenfold. Let it go! Drop the pointless quarrelling and embrace your brothers and sisters, for they are innocent just as you are.

Let us discuss this on a more practical level. When the workplace supervisor (or mate, or parent, or child) says or does something that sets you off, here is a fine plan of action: retreat in calm fashion. Do not react. Keep a pleasant demeanor as you exit the space, heavy with potential turmoil. Do nothing in haste. Go about your business until the day is done.

Once in the quiet of your abode, call that soul to your mind. Remember that all souls are connected. The absence of form cannot diminish the power and importance of this exercise. You must be sincere. Do you intend peace?.. then proceed. If you intend harm, drop the exercise and wait until dreams of revenge cease to taunt the mind and fall away. Revenge is an illusion, for the arrows you fling from your trusty bow return to you in full force.

Let us begin. Be still and request of this soul his full participation. Have no distractions. Let the space be Holy… a conduit for Higher Learning. Close your eyes and envision a simple room in your mind. Now see this individual approaching. Open the door and invite him to come in and sit down. Now take a breath. You have held much inside. It is your chance to speak. We promise you, this is a safe place. Welcome the anger and tears as they bubble to the surface.

Some may find this assignment daunting. When you have difficulty releasing suppressed emotions, ask yourself this: *"What am I afraid of? What is my fear relating to this person or memory?"* The ego may convince you that the question lacks merit. It will say fear has no part in it. But we urge you to silence the persistent gnat and think again. If you do not love this brother, then you fear him. So explore that place and do not leave until you know the answer.

Express all to this soul. Hold nothing back. Once you have done so, allow *him* to speak. Sit quietly as he reveals to you what is in his heart. This phase of the process is quite astounding. We will not give away the story's ending. Just know that you have entered into something sacred. There follows a special closeness... a bond between you that strengthens with each passing day.

As your meeting comes to a close, thank this soul for his contribution and release him to go on his way. We note that this practice can and should be used for every troubled relationship, even when it involves a soul who has passed on. Remember that the body is a mere vehicle, nothing more. It is the clay... formed and reformed, and ever-changing.

Honor what you have done here, and use this same process for all wounds in need of repair. This is the soul contract… a life lesson agreed upon well in advance. Both student and teacher work together to complete their studies, and once learned, they part. Or perhaps they will embark on another adventure together. We encourage you to open your mind and allow limitation and conditioning to fall away. Begin to see relationships in a new light, and you will no longer feel threatened by anyone, under any circumstance.

You have met with your brother and allowed love to wash away your imagined disharmony. The question is, what will you do with your desire for conflict, now that there is peace between you? A very good question, indeed! Continue to seek our counsel, and we will happily show you how to fill the void.

Chapter 2:
Prosperity and Wealth

There is nothing that humans strive to obtain with greater zeal and enthusiasm than monetary wealth. From our perspective, it is a spectacle. One would think by the looks of things that it is sustenance or required fare to permit a soul to advance to the next level. They arrive in droves, trans-like, eyes glazed over, drooling at the sight of it… the paper bill you worship, stamped with your Father's name upon it.

Many have risked death to possess it. We can assure you curious humans, the currency you have chosen and the way in which you engage it, is of no more value than the parchment [paper] it is printed on. In fact, it can easily lead astray. In its current state, it is potentially harmful and can cause great detriment to the soul who accumulates large quantities, for it lacks energy. Without spiritual grounding, it is lifeless and stops the natural flow of things.

There is an inherent yearning for loving expression in all matter. Your current method of exchange is disconnected and hollow. It senses its own lack of wholeness. The system is out of balance – in need of healing. Humans sense it too.

This is why monetary wealth often causes hording, selfishness, and greed.

The earliest uses of money as an exchange were much more intelligent. Brothers offered their wares and bartered for the best price with animal pelts and coins of gold. Do you recall gatherings with friends and acquaintances, presenting gifts and useful items to one another for trade? The hand-made treasures were especially significant. Was it not a joyous occasion? You have given away your traditions and are left with something you believe to be improved, but it is devoid of life energy. Your choices save you time, but what is the ultimate cost?

Modern practices have you spending your day in tall buildings, sitting at desks, staring at lifeless screens with fingers clicking away on keys. You are like robots. You watch the clock and go through the motions of your daily routine, relishing every break, looking for snacks and other distractions, and making idle conversation to relieve the continuous boredom. The much-anticipated whistle blows and you are free at last!

How do you spend the remainder of your day?.. clutching your beloved electronic gadgets, affixed to your massive television sets. You see this as a great technological feat and a testament to man's progress. But how empty your lives have become!

You rarely gaze into the eyes of another or shake the warm hand of a stranger. Cursive writing has become a lost art along with so many other creative forms of expression. Fine baking skills are a thing of the past, as is the nightly family gathering... telling stories and playing music together. The harvest is left to machinery as you stuff your mouths with unnatural concoctions and elixirs until you cannot breathe. The excess food is then thrown away... discarded as refuse, rather than shared with those in need.

And so continues your quest for greater acquisition of wealth, land, jewels, and other pointless things. Hear us when we tell you, they are mere trinkets. The ground you walk upon cannot be possessed... neither the air you breathe nor the ocean you swim in. Do you own the clouds?.. or the rainbow? How do you prevent the birds from flying across your designated borders, marked with gravestones?

For a moment, can you imagine your earthly home, joyfully shared by those you love? Many larger homes in the southernmost territories and less modern communities and villages throughout the world are occupied by three generations. From grandparents to grandchildren, all gather at the dinner table, sharing lively conversation over a bounty harvested from the fields. It would be unthinkable to cordon off sections of the house, establishing boundaries, charging fares, conducting searches, and jailing trespassers. Can you see the absurdity of your current system?

Ownership is a strange concept to advanced souls. They understand it goes against nature. God created a world for sharing. But brother fought with brother and made suits of armor. They became soldiers. Dear Ones, the only possessions of value are inherent… God-given…. never to be lost. You must give up your greed and hoarding, in order to have. That is true wealth. The giving heart is the winner of this game.

We are attempting to encourage you to see the futility in your reasoning. The best gauge of decent conduct is the sense of joy you feel. Engaging in any act of kindness produces good feelings that linger on long after. It is the gift that expands the heart. When one focuses entirely on gain of personal possessions, you have excluded your brother. Without him, there can be no satisfaction. More importantly, there can be no peace.

So you might ask, *"How does one become prosperous by giving things away?"* Here is how it works: the very act of surrendering, of letting go of attachment, opens the floodgates. The river of wealth is redirected, flowing freely, right to your doorstep. The coins pile high as you marvel at your abundance. But the giving heart sees the coins from a Higher Perspective.

The supply is a resource. It is capable of tremendous power… to be used in service. This is the understanding you are missing in your current state of blatant inequity. It is a disease that has spread throughout the world. Starving people are the result. Do you not see it? You believe the solutions are unattainable or lay dormant in a distant land. But the answer is right in front of you, clear as your image in the mirror. It is your great struggle to conceal and feign ignorance that expends most of your energy. That is why you often feel tired.

You are holding back an ocean of wisdom in exchange for the reality you have chosen. You have decided that your brother is your enemy… that life is unjust and that God has forsaken you. And so you design the flawed structure to resemble your vision of lack or greed, and play the part of a hapless victim or conqueror.

Let us now repair this belief in lack, victimhood, and greed. The first thing you must do is forgive. And who are you to forgive?... There is only Self, so begin there. If your brother has accumulated wealth, rejoice! For his blessings are yours. Do not forget that. If you harbor feelings of jealousy, you will prevent your own flow of wealth.

Now share your possessions with those in need. You may think *you* are the one in need and therefore have nothing to spare. But that is exactly the mentality that will hold you prisoner and continue the pattern of poverty and gluttony. Know that you have everything you need, right now. This is key to transforming the old belief system. Be grateful for what you have. Stop waiting for something to shift, to correct itself in the future… or for some grand windfall to come.

You are the designer of your life. It is an active process. Do not sit idly by, expecting things to change. Look around you, and give thanks to the Father... to Source. Do this every day. Make it a habit. This simple practice will transform your thoughts and create genuine wealth.

Have you considered what you will do with your newly acquired millions? You have spent your entire life, and perhaps many lifetimes, planning for destitution and hardship. Your language is peppered with caustic wanting. Drop this destructive habit and be watchful of your words, as they possess great power. You must now create a new vision. What dreams lie unfulfilled? How will you help your brothers in need? This is the way through.

Begin the process and never look back. Doubt has no place in the demonstration of wealth. Remember that you cannot climb the mountain alone. You must take your brothers and sisters with you. Do this and you will reach the summit together. This is steadfast and true prosperity. Let go of your attachment to earthly possessions and embrace the beauty that is all around you. It is the Father's creation... everything you see. It is all Love.

Chapter 3:
Honoring the Heart

*I*t is puzzling that you, Dear Humans, need guidance in this area. For the heart is the core and cornerstone of who you are. Yet you have suppressed your essence for so long, the concept of listening or quiet reflection seems foreign to you. If you but understood and put into practice this one principle, you would require no books, and never again need advice from any source for any reason. The world would [will] cease to exist because you will have overcome it.

You would have learned all you need to transcend limited thinking. Fear and hate would fall away, as their engagement would have no purpose and hold no interest. Effortlessly, you would ascend to the next dimension, with peace in your hearts. You would long for nothing, filled to the brim with joy. And you would lay down the heavy body as you soar to the skies and beyond. If you will allow it, the heart can lead you. This is the key that unlocks every door.

The world you have invented is just that... an invention. It is not real. And herein lies the crux of your schoolwork. It is your job to see past illusion and return to your true nature. The path you have chosen is full of potholes...

roadblocks at every turn. You have become dejected and filled with doubt. But the answer is right in front of you.

Take a deep breath. Now close your eyes. Be still and listen. What do you hear? The heart is speaking to you. The way is clear at last. Let us look at this process from a different perspective.

We begin with the human language and its tendency to veer you off course. As you speak, listen to your words. Observe your daily habits and the conversations you participate in. You rely on television and radio personalities to report events around the world. But have you thought about where these individuals get their scripts? Would the dialogue be different had they traveled to those far away places and met with the local people there?

Let us look at an aspect of your cultural habits. Have you regarded the chatter that takes place in your office lunchrooms? You discuss favored television shows and the actions of make-believe people in conjured up situations. You do not realize it, but this pointless activity gives rise to the antics of a backseat driver. Even the more serious events that make headlines are motivated to sway and rally support toward a particular agenda. Truly, there are many layers to your imaginary world.

We now present you with an assignment. In your conversation, listen for the familiar sounds that form words and trigger recognition. You are inclined to react without thought. Let us now disengage the autopilot feature. The next time you hear a phrase, allow the syllables to float about as they enter and exit the eardrum cavity. Do not respond in kneejerk fashion. Rather, be content to form no opinion at all. Take no side.

This is an exercise in non-judgment. It will not come easily for most humans. But the rewards are immeasurable. When you do respond, pay close attention to the words you have chosen and the emotion behind them. This exercise is especially beneficial to the citizens of your country at this pivotal time in history. You are beginning to see the futility of façade and pretense. It has revealed itself as manipulation. What your world is hankering for is honesty and heartfelt connection.

Have you observed the many food vendors that dot the land and fill the streets? You flock to your markets in search of something but you do not know what it is. So you fill your carts and bags with every item conceivable, hoping to solve the problem once and for all... but to no avail. The hunger persists. Let us delve deeper into this important issue so you can move beyond the deception.

Physical hunger – the cry for sustenance – is a normal function of a newborn baby. The bonding between mother and child is imperative for both, offering far more than nutrition. It is contentment that surpasses and quells all yearning. When one reaches adulthood, the needs of the body wane. Problems begin to surface when the grown child feels that pit in the stomach. The desire for nurturing and comfort gnaw at the gut in much the same way as hunger or thirst. But the grown body needs almost nothing to sustain itself. The notion seems radical, contrary to modern day consensus thinking. This is where the confusion lies.

Yet unfulfilled, the mind grows irritable and begins to lust for attention and praise. This emotional ache is mistaken for a need for food. So you stuff yourselves with an endless array of culinary temptations until you are nearly ill. Over consumption is epidemic in your [Western] culture. It is the cause of much discomfort and disease. Again, we return to the basic flaw in the foundation – the belief in abandonment and a forsaken Son of God.

This bears repeating. The true hunger you feel is your longing for reunion… to heal the separation of mother and child… of God and His Son. You are unaware of it. The memory is buried deep in the folds of the brain's cortex. Nearly everything you think and do stems from this one faulty belief. This must be corrected in order to bring peace and wholeness to the weary Sons and Daughters of Israel.

This leads us to the heart, which is the true navigator. So let us begin there. Again, we ask you to still the mind. Take a deep breath and exhale slowly. Let go of all worries. They have no meaning whatsoever. If you will accept this, just long enough to create a new belief, you will have overcome the world. We are here to show you how to do just that.

Now close your eyes. Speak to each and every concern. What is underneath the fear? If you are unsure, ask for assistance.

Do not rush this process. You are discovering a new form of communication… one that leads to the vast pool of Higher Consciousness. Now ask a different question, this time of the heart: *"How may I honor you this day?"* Wait in the silence for the answer. You may hear a simple phrase or a mere word… something like, *nature… water… sun… rest… music…* or *forgive.* Make note and fulfill your promise to accommodate the heart's desires. Take it seriously, just as you would a request from a close friend, your mate, a colleague, or your child.

At this point, the ego will begin to rant and rave that the answer is too simple. Remember that the ego loves conflict and false remedies… those that block your path and delay your good. It enjoys nothing more than to lead you astray, turning you around and around until you have lost your way. That is its ultimate goal… to make you fearful, needy, and miserable. The ego is truly idiotic. Once you recognize its predictable foolishness, you will cease to trust it.

Ego has no new tricks up the sleeve… nothing more to tempt you with. Just the same old stale routine that it tries to conceal with shiny new wrapping paper. You anticipate fire and brimstone – my, how the sparks fly from the magician's wand. You tremble with fear. But ego is growing tired. Do you not sense its inevitable demise? The end is coming, just as you have imagined.

But no death can come to a Child of God. What you observe is shedding of the old skin like that of a snake. Do not fear this essential process. It is the end of illusion and chaos. You slumber but the Great Awakening is upon you. It will soon be a time of unrivaled joy and profound peace.

This is what we recommend. Give the heart full reign over your lives this very day. Start small so you can understand the significance of its vital role. We give you this example. After a particularly difficult work shift, ask the heart again, *"How may I honor you?"* Then wait for the answer. Make a conscientious effort to fulfill its wishes. You may be guided to take up a hobby or make peace with a neighbor. Perhaps you feel stuck in the choices you have made. Have you considered leaving the current job for something more rewarding? Honoring the Heart reveals the open window.

You have yet to understand the importance of this simple act of accommodation. We tell you this: allowing the heart to lead is necessary for your soul's development and transcendence. Consult the heart when there is tension in a relationship. Perhaps you are nearing the end of your study time together. Humans are inclined to cling to the familiar. But lingering in the hallway after the school bell has rung merely delays the start of the next class. So let it go.

If you cannot hear the whispering of your heart, take a break and try again the following evening. Make sure the space is free of distraction. Your intention must be sincere. In the weeks and months that follow, continue to make small changes in your routine that reflect engagement with your heart center. You will begin to see shifts in your thinking and choices. As you devote more of your time to this assignment, you will experience greater joy. Stress will abate, and decisions will come easy. If you want to be truly happy, surrender to the will of the heart!

Chapter 4:
Body Wisdom

This chapter will offer another opportunity for you to undo what you believe, this time as it relates to the human form. The body is a magnificent creation. Superior in design, it is a wondrous collaboration with but one purpose: to allow Spirit to explore the physical plane. Your knowledge of the human body is so very limited, and what you think you know is obscured and only half true. Let us now guide you as we examine this expansive area of misinformation and confusion.

You do not understand how the body works. The very foundation of what you believe to be true is flawed, and so your approach is flawed as well. It is as if you are peering through a fractured looking glass. What you see are independent body parts that appear separate, disjointed, and autonomous. But you could not be more mistaken. Every organ, every muscle and neurotransmitter… every molecule, atom, and tinier particle still… speak to one another continuously.

Have you observed the grace and exquisite perfection of a flock of seabirds, circling above the ocean? Swiftly they rise and suddenly change direction, descending and then turning sharply… never colliding but moving in harmony as one. It is lovely to watch, is it not? Do they need instruction or assistance to accomplish this feat? You know they do not. So how do we convince you, Dear Humans, that the body needs no help in order to reestablish and maintain its equilibrium?

Here is what you must know about the body. Unlike the birds in flight, the body must navigate past numerous obstacles that you have managed to place before it, interfering with its homeostatic balance. Impure foods, defiled air and water, and corrosive thoughts, pollute the body until it can scarcely recognize itself. Communication is reduced to a level nearly inaudible. Enter modern medical aspirations and the onset of highly intricate surgical manipulations, followed by an assortment of tablets and elixirs of questionable value.

You humans are so trusting in this area. You would fare better to ask questions. There is so much to sort through. Let us help you determine what can be discarded and what should be retained. We will provide you with a tool so that you will always know what is best for you in any situation from this point forward. Are you now willing to expand your vision and let go of the old belief? If so, then continue the course.

Here is your first clue: how do you feel on your present regimen? Do you have boundless energy? Are you giddy and hardly able to contain your joy? Do you dance freely, without a care as to who might be watching? When you gaze in the mirror, is there a youthfulness and a pleasant, winning smile in the reflection? Are you content?.. in need of nothing, with a burning desire to lift your brothers so that they may also share in your celebration? If our words fall flat and stir nothing in you, then sadly, you have not experienced this natural, intrinsic jubilation we speak of in quite some time.

You have been miserable for so long, Dear Ones. This is the prison you have made. You curse it, but who is the designer? It is time to set yourselves free. Through blame and ignorance, you built the walls, brick by brick. But it is no more solid than a hologram. You fear the unknown. Take courage. We are with you.

We call on you now. It is time. Be willing to venture out beyond the confined space you have become so accustomed to. Reach for the key, residing in the deep, dusty pocket, and unlock the heavy door. Now step through the doorway and embrace your freedom. We will spell this out for you.

Let us demonstrate our point with this scene from your daily lives. You run yourselves ragged, darting about in all directions, always in a hurry, not paying full attention to anything or anyone. This is your routine. Stress is a daily occurrence and you consider it to be normal. You gobble down your meals and gab on your electronic devices. You work late into the night, and take your pills to sleep, to wake, or to settle your stomachs. Your automobiles crowd the roads of your bustling cities, filled with passersby, whom you hardly acknowledge.

In the evening, you collapse in your easy chairs and stare blankly at oversized screens displaying thousands of moving images. You have convinced yourselves that you are enjoying this activity. But you do not remember the joy of creating and dancing... of self-expression. You have forgotten how to laugh. Why else would you need recordings of coached laughter to accompany your humorous television shows?

We will refresh your memory. The child, yet untrained and free of programming, laughs and plays, stumbles and picks himself up, without a care. He learns and explores freely, without judgment. The child's body, unless otherwise directed by soul contract, is healthy and vibrant... yet untainted by the world around him. But years of unloving and disrespect take their toll.

We apprise you humans – the damage can be reversed. Only disbelief can prevent the body from renewing and repairing itself. Do you find this statement unprecedented? We assure you, your power to heal or to make sick is far greater than you have imagined.

It is easier for you to believe in the healing qualities of a tiny pill than your own God-given ability to manifest and heal. Why is that? We marvel at this anomaly and apparent glitch in the machinery that is the human mind. Truly, it is something you have adopted and not authentic to your nature. You fear your power and recoil at the thought of using it. Will you consider relinquishing just a smidgen of doubt? Allow us to show you what you are capable of and once the demonstration is complete, you may resume your limited existence as you see fit.

Here is your assignment: for just one evening, turn off all electronics. Take a walk in the moonlight and gaze up at the stars. If you have trouble seeing them in your congested cities full of electric light, obtain a high-powered telescope for viewing. The stars are ancient, Holy Beings. They have guided you on your travels for thousands of years. You have forgotten these sacred scholars, replacing them with magnetic pointers.

Do you remember earth wisdom emanating from the mountainous rock? Crystals served you well for centuries until recent discoveries convinced you there were other tools more efficient. What you do not realize in your endless quest for one-upmanship is that you have cast aside aides of particular value. They hold the essence of your ancestors… of ancient wisdom. These Guides are gifted, skillful in the art of design and engineering. They are here to help you during your stay on earth.

Your decision to turn away from these sacred teachers has caused you much pain and angst. Your pain is self-inflicted, though you cannot see it. We are here, Dear Children. We watch over you, ready to assist or intervene if necessary. You deem yourselves orphans, but your Father Lives! Even when you are "lost" at sea for days on end, we offer you comfort, and help to restore your Faith.

You ask, *"Why am I here?"* You do not remember signing up for the class. Alone and afraid, you worry that you have been forgotten. But no Child of God is ever forgotten. Your Father has seen to it. Every sojourner has his name sewn in the fabric of the Sacred Tapestry.

We offer you another option to help you rediscover your playful nature: find a shop for youngsters and allow yourselves the gift of a child's toy. Peruse the aisles to see what catches your eye. Select just the right one… a game perhaps, or modeling clay or paints… something you once loved long ago. Take your toy home and unabashedly delight in the time you spend engaging in playtime. If you are so inclined, invite your housemates to join in. Now observe with astonishment how this subtle change in your routine begins to unleash the willing and eager child residing within.

Do not be surprised if your chronic health problems begin to disappear. The greatest threat to mankind's continued presence on planet earth is not war nor pestilence. These are secondary to the root cause. It is boredom. You have run out of things to thrill yourselves with. You have built your towers and now you have begun to tumble them, just to create a new challenge for yourselves.

You must complete your studies, as they are necessary for your evolution and transcendence. Here is one more suggestion to help liberate the stiff outer shell that has seized your energetic body: visit a music store. Try out the many instruments on display until one of them begins to resonate with the vibration of your soul. It does not matter if you can play the instrument or not. Again, we appeal to your adventurous side and ask that you make no judgment about this exercise until it is complete.

Make room for this musical addition to your home. Have the family gather round. Invite them to join you. The ego will not like what we have proposed. In fact, the mere sound of it is truly repugnant to the ego. But that is predictable, because if it allowed you to be happy, the ego would endanger its own survival. We recommend that you disregard it for the duration of this exercise.

You are beginning to see the various ways in which you can rebalance the mind and body. We will now address some specific symptoms in order to drive home our point. Let us say you are experiencing symptoms of cold or flu. The body aches. The throat is inflamed, accompanied by congestion and fever. The typical human mindset is geared toward outside assistance. So you seek counsel from a purveyor of medicine. It is all quite logical in your mind. The masses believe this approach offers a reputable source of information and cure all... and you believe it too.

The practice of medicine is based on the premise that the body acts independently of the mind… is irrational at times, susceptible to the elements, and will eventually break down and succumb to disease. It is further surmised that the body lacks the intelligence to correct its own maladies and afflictions. The body's wisdom in producing symptoms is ignored and dismissed entirely. So a medically-trained professional steps in to cut and patch where needed to remove the cells gone haywire.

The body is regarded by medical science as a volatile, unpredictable conglomerate of tissue, bones and blood, apt to lose its way and due harm to its host with little warning. Once the problematic areas have been identified, war is declared on the body. Medicines are prescribed. If the patient's health worsens, surgical procedures are soon to follow. We ask you this… what is your strategy when the patient's health does *not* improve? Oddly, you humans continue on the same path, following the same routine. Why would you expect a successful outcome when signs indicate otherwise?

This is most baffling to us. It seems you are most intent on proving the body's ignorance and maladaptation at any cost… even if it means your own life. When did you turn away and denounce the body's inherent wisdom in exchange for the remedies of peddlers? Indeed, it has cost you dearly.

For centuries, you have denied the body… stifled and suppressed its powers to heal. You line up in throngs to collect your medications and apothecary. These are not benign compounds, Dear Ones. The body is a perfectly designed, harmonious, living machine that requires clean fuel. You would not dare to defile your prized automobiles with impurities, so why do you not exhibit the same care with respect to your precious bodies?

We now present you with the answer to the riddle of how to address symptoms while respecting the body. If you recall from the previous chapter, the heart speaks to you, and you must listen in order to maintain health of mind and body. This is part of the very same discussion. The body is wise and needs no help to correct any imbalance. What it does need is the removal of any and all obstacles blocking its way. Herein lies the challenge.

You must decipher what it means to remove the obstacle. We will explain so there is no confusion. First, you must be clear on what exactly constitutes an obstacle. So be still and ask the body. Do not rush to treat for any reason, in any fashion.

You must understand this concept fully: no outside interference can affect a body without permission. Once consent is given, effort, sometimes great, is required to reverse its momentum. The seed that grew the tree of self-hatred, which opened the door to disease, must be identified. This is a deep concept, so allow yourselves time to absorb and process it.

As you take this first step, merely acknowledge that all beings agree to all the circumstances of their lives, including acts of seeming happenstance. Truly, there are no coincidences, and no mistakes. There are many layers to this truth, so we will commence for now with an overview to further our discussion. Any hindrance to maintaining health must be identified by the body first in order to clear it.

Follow the same guidelines as before. Take a deep breath and close your eyes. Be still. Now ask for guidance. Then listen for the answer. Keep repeating this process nightly until you begin to hear the inner voice. The body will speak to you in simple words, easy to comprehend. It will say such things as, *sun, water, quiet, warmth,* and *rest.* You would be wise to follow its directive.

Your mind may not want such a simple answer. Humans are quite accustomed to making the simple, complex. We cannot tell you how many times we have witnessed your clever turning around of circumstances into a rat's nest of confusion. What could once be solved with ease becomes a task nearly impossible to complete. This is a fascinating aspect of your humanness… the desire to create problems… to break things, just to know the satisfaction of fixing them.

If you followed the steps we have laid out, you will have listened to your body, and done precisely as instructed. If you are a good student, you allowed the body to rest. The country doctor of old believed in bed rest for his patients. That was the remedy he prescribed for a plethora of ailments. This is a reliable form of antidote even today. But one thing we must point out is the vast difference in your diets.

Farmers planted and harvested a variety of crops, without chemical aides. Meals were made with fresh ingredients, grown within or nearby town limits. This is not the harvest you know today. You must make corrections if you desire good health. Begin with a natural diet of fresh plants, herbs, grains, and seeds. Learn to recognize natural bounty from the fields. Man-made foodstuffs are unnatural and contain many questionable substances. Remember that each species has its own unique requirements.

There is much discussion about what constitutes a useful and appropriate diet for humankind. We will refrain from saying more to prevent you from jumping ahead in your studies. It is up to each individual to discover it for himself. When you are ready, look to your cousin in the Animal Kingdom and that will reveal all.

Know too, that the body is affected by all things exposed to it. Frightening images on the screens of your television sets penetrate and permeate the mind's eye. Once held there, the mind begins to dwell on and recreate those images in various arenas. Hence, if you desire peace, it is unwise to expose the mind to conflict. We remind you, Dear Ones… violence begets violence. Be willing to view all aspects of [animal] food preparation, from field to market, in its entirety. The walls of these structures are solid and allow no light. So do your research, and make it thorough.

Remember that you can change nothing until you agree to look upon the thing you detest. There can be no peace as long as a living creature is targeted for harm. Activities of a contemptible nature have been shrouded from your sight. But you are aware of injustice no matter how deeply hidden. Do you truly wish for peace on your planet? Then look honestly at the many expressions of violence that are all around you and be willing to take responsibility for your part in them.

We will now clear up your misunderstanding of how one act or event is followed by another. We are referring to what you term *cause and effect*. This chapter is the appropriate place for this segment, as we will be discussing the body to make our point. It is a continuation of our earlier discussion about the perfection of life. There are no coincidences. But rather there is mutual agreement. What we demonstrate now will help you fully grasp this concept.

During the course of its daily functions, the body must purge waste in order to remain in good standing. Your modern diets and stress-filled lifestyles are contributing factors, not to be ignored. When the body is struggling to rid itself of the accumulation of debris, movement of the body is essential as well as rest from all activity. You spend little time relaxing outdoors in the sun or taking leisurely walks. Here is where you must pay close attention...

The body needs assistance when the normal points of depository are overwhelmed. So it asks for help from an outside source and a helper is enlisted. If this is an insect, it will sting or bite in order to help create a point of release for the body. A door may be of assistance as you stub your toe while opening it, or your teammate may knock into you during a scrimmage. Depending on the severity, the body may be laid up for several hours, days, or weeks while the toxins are allowed to exit. All of these scenarios underscore the symbiotic nature and connectedness of every living thing.

As you can see, cause and effect is much more intelligent and synergistic than you have imagined. It is easy to misread all you see. A nail left by a roofer just happened to pierce the foot of an unsuspecting passerby. And you think, *"If he had just walked 3 centimeters to the left, it would not have happened."* You watch your news programs and are filled with fear. You see a plane crash and vow to never fly again, thinking that will protect you from a world so unpredictable. But it is not as you think. We must explain this now so you will be at peace.

Here is the truth: the souls onboard were aware of what was to come and they agreed to participate in the lesson.

You must trust that there is a grand and perfect objective, of which you are a part. As students, your job is to understand the lesson and learn from it so you will not have to repeat it. The Children of God are meant to help one another. So if you are in need, ask for help. And if you have plenty, then share your surplus.

When there is loss, give comfort to those in pain. Your world of duality is apt to confuse. You know that all events have purpose, but that does not mean you disregard the emotional aspects of your being. You are human. It would be thoughtless not to recognize the effect it has on emotional beings to lose a loved one.

Hence, it is a unique place to be… a soul in a body, with the wisdom and beauty instilled in you as a Child of God, and at the same time, being frightened and bewildered by the ego's goading. It is your job to navigate through the confusion. You must work together to emerge from your dream state.

As our discussion draws to a close, you are beginning to see how interrelated all things are… body, mind, and even the chapters in this compilation. Clear the mind and allow the body to do its repair work. There is nothing more to its complete restoration. We are fully aware of the economic changes and transfer of power these ideas, once implemented, will foster. Upheaval and confusion may reign for a time, but is it not better than what you have now? Sickness of mind and body runs rampant.

Anger and impatience is a way of life for a great number of you. And what is joyous about that? Life is to be savored and relished… partaken of with wild abandon! Far too many of God's Children are sad… eyes fixed to the ground, as they muddle through their day. Fearful of bad news, you aspire for nothing more than to keep the details of your unhappy existence copasetic… wishing only to maintain the status quo. Truly, you are not living as your loving Father in Heaven intended.

We urge you to begin today by spending time in the silence. Sit quietly and tune out the static. Just a few moments spent in contemplation will begin to awaken the knowledge you hold deep inside. You already know the answer to every question you could possibly ask on this earthly plane. Stop looking outside yourselves! It serves no purpose, but to delay your growth and soul's development.

This is our suggestion… give thanks this very minute for the body, no matter what condition it appears to be in. You are the commander of your vessel. So take the wheel and begin to focus on the power and beauty inherent in the perfect Son that is you. Let go of the programming. Retire the magnifying glass, with its harsh perspective, and set your gaze upon the Heavens. That is the perspective we aim to give you. It is where all the threads of the tapestry come together in blissful harmony.

Chapter 5:
The Intelligence of Animals

*T*here is a diverse and expansive world around you, teeming with life. Humans, through ignorance and fear, have come to see the world as something to be conquered. You are filled with pride when you tame a beast, and feel victorious in the act of slaying. The heads of countless animals hang on the walls of your hunting lodges. But you have forgotten the story of your beginnings together. We will refresh your memory.

You were new in the world, exploring the jungles, foraging, seeking shelter from the rains. You were alone, until you saw a critter. For a moment, you beheld one another... each of you curious about the other. You shared your berries and seeds with the critter. Humans walked the earth with every living thing. The climate was warm and there was plenty to eat. But you soon grew curious about life beyond Eden.

You ventured past the jungles – east, to the desert. The summer heat burned your skin. Food was scarce. The winter months were harsh and you nearly froze. Ice and snow covered the barren land. After a lightning storm, you discovered fire. Without abundant plant life and with hunger in your belly, you began to look upon animals, your kindred, as marks. You eyed their meaty legs and fur and feathers… seeing them as warmth for the body and your next meal. You set a trap, and a hare fell prey. And so the friendship between you began to crumble. Fear was born, and paradise was lost.

Distrust and suspicion set in. The camaraderie you once shared came to an end. It was a time of great sadness for all. As man hunted beast, the beasts retaliated. Animals turned on one another and began to hunt and kill each other. Every act of violence… every attack between and among the species, came from this crucial turning point in man's evolution.

Fear grew rampant as predator chased prey. Anger and suffering filled the air. The sound of their cries was heard by all… circling the planet a thousand times over. The killing raged, sometimes for food and other times for spite. It spread to every corner of the earth. Man fabricated a better killing tool… sling shot, bow and arrow, axe, and gun, to improve his kill ratios. The animals adapted too by growing fangs and claws.

The Children of God wept when they saw what they had done. For some humans, the pain was too great. So they closed their hearts and pushed their sensitive natures deep down. They hid themselves behind the mask of pride and boastfulness.

Humans told many lies to justify their behavior. They convinced themselves that animals were brainless and therefore meant to be eaten. As the centuries passed, killing of animals became a way of life. Pelts that were once used for warmth were fashioned to adorn the rich, and the practice continues today. Flesh, skin, bones, organs, feathers, fur, tusks, feet, tails, and bodily fluids all are prized throughout the world. Humble beginnings transformed into a vast form of commerce.

Domestication of animals soon followed. Animals were selected and bred for a variety of uses. Some plowed the fields… others carried heavy loads or pulled carts. Animals were milked, and their coats were made ready or spun into yarn. Many were killed for their flesh or used in rituals as sacrifice. Modern agriculture has taken this idea and pushed it to its limit. Animals are barely able to stand under the pressure. The system is headed for collapse. Trust us when we tell you, it [collapse] is a blessing.

In recent times, the killing of animals has gone underground. The houses that slaughter are windowless. It is civilized and considered progress to hide the details of an act of killing. But that is precisely how this injurious practice continues. You have blinders on, Dear Ones.

You have turned away, refusing to look upon the pain on their faces for fear you will burst into tears at the sight. You know it is wrong to take a life. Your Father decreed it and your Brother Yeshua was a living example. We ask you,

Dear Children… are you now ready to look upon the horror that will break your hearts?

A heart that is numb and cold must first be broken before it can be resuscitated. We give you our promise… you will not perish as you take this most important first step. Rather, you will begin to truly live in harmony with all of God's Creations. Every creature great and small is a part of you. That is why you are filled with remorse when you harm another. A part of you remembers your connection to every living thing.

We want you to understand the injury you cause to self when you take a life. You have decided that one type of killing is necessary for food, while another kind of killing is worthy of celebration and medals, and still another condemns a man to prison. We tell you truly, it is all murder. We will now say what you need to hear regarding this very difficult subject…

There is no death. We have stated this earlier in the text, but it bears repeating. It must be understood as it pertains to our discussion. There can be no death, and this means all inhabitants of the earth. Again, this is a many-layered concept and will take time to comprehend.

You do not die, but the body's existence ends abruptly when there is premeditation. The soul must enter a new body to resume his studies. Remember that the classwork is required… it cannot be omitted. It can only be postponed.

Each course is specifically laid out for an intended purpose. You may ask, what is the harm in ending the life of form?

It is a fair question. The answer is, the damage you do to self is held in the DNA of the cells until it is made clean and restored. The punishment you inflict upon yourselves is far greater than a lifetime spent in a wretched prison cell in the most deplorable of conditions.

We will help you by proving our point. Do you recall a time when you hated? You held a fellow human in utter disregard and wished him the worst of fates. You wished him a painful death. Take heart, Dear Ones… you have all wished this at one time or another. Of this, we are certain because you are descendants of Cain. You looked upon him as evil, but you are afraid to look in the mirror… afraid to know yourselves, because you believe it will unleash the demon, and you will run through the streets when the moon is full, preying on the helpless.

The stories were told to you when you were children, and as you grew into adulthood, your fear turned inward and mutated into self-hatred. Not knowing how to expel it, you lashed out, killing the tiniest of beasts… the insects. Your scientists have placed so many of the world's problems upon these bold and brave creatures. They are the hardest of workers ever to inhabit your planet. But that is not how you view them. They are considered pests and annihilated by the thousands every day.

So few of you humans understand that the taking of a life, no matter how minuscule, correlates to death of a living being. Its impact is not to be taken lightly. Again, your false assumption that insects lack intelligence and therefore have no place, is the lie you tell yourselves in order to justify the act. It is deliberate.

You may ask, how important can an ant be? We answer it this way… very important to the ant family. His family is no less important than yours. That will be a challenge for many of you to accept… that all life is sacred. The taking of one life, no matter how insignificant it may seem, does great harm to the human psyche.

Our discussion is bound to trigger a defensive response. Allow our words to sink in on their own volition. You must not push yourselves to grasp its meaning prematurely. If what we have said causes you to reevaluate your choices, then that is sufficient for now. There is a time for all things. Be grateful for wisdom. It serves you well.

Let us now continue. The question to ask is, how can humans reconnect with their fellow earth dwellers? It is rather simple. Begin by observing how you treat a treasured friend. You are considerate and look out for his welfare. If this friend is human, you inquire about his happiness and health, and whatever else concerns him. You spend time together, doing things you both enjoy. Now take this same premise and transfer it to an animal.

Canines make wonderful companions because they are joyous. They love to play and make humans laugh as do dolphins and select members of all species that interact with Mankind. Other animals also make good pets if they have an interest in living among humans. Felines are included in this group as are many bird species. But take notice of their behavior. Felines are less apt to be satisfied with enclosures or restraints of any kind. Specific bird species may be content to live indoors. But the majority of them will not find joy in a caged existence.

If you have developed a relationship with one of these special animals, begin to see him in a new light. Make a concerted effort to connect with him, on his level. What exactly does he need and what makes him happy? Spouting orders or tossing leftovers on the floor is not respectful. You would not treat a dear friend in this manner.

Just as we made our point earlier about the human body's need for healthy food, we say again that every species requires a specific diet to maintain health. The packaged mixes of uncertain, less than wholesome ingredients can do more harm than good.

Make sure to provide for all of their needs, not just nutritional. Humans tend to cut short the time they spend with their animal companions. Animals thrive on exploring the wild. They prefer a warm bed and food in their bellies, but do not deprive them of joyful exploration. Domestic animals have not forgotten roaming free and the excitement of the chase. They act out their frustration in a variety of ways. Accommodate their wild side and you will see undesirable habits begin to vanish.

Can you provide this creature with an enjoyable, healthy environment? Discover his likes and dislikes. Humans are notorious for acquiring possessions, to dress and adorn themselves and their abodes. Animals are often made to fit in a particular space like furniture… paid attention to only as time permits. Try your best, Dear Ones, to avoid this practice.

Some members of a genus or family may find human companionship acceptable and even desirable, while another member of the same family will be quite miserable with the arrangement. Pay close attention to this, especially in your zoos and other animal facilities in which breeding programs and visitor attendance is part of the dealings. You must honor these animal ambassadors by arranging for their release once they begin to show signs of fatigue. Do not force them to remain in confinement beyond that point. It is easy to become complacent… blindsided by the promise of uninterrupted funding. You sentence these animals to a life that is meaningless, leading to slow decay, disease, and eventual death.

Now let us discuss animals in the role of support in shouldering life lessons for their human counterparts. The incarnation may present a particularly heavy lesson in which extra support is needed. An animal will come forward to volunteer for the assignment. The bond that forms between animal and human in these circumstances is unique and quite special, indeed. Once the invitation is sent out, a soul replies and joins his human. From that point on, they work as a team to solve problems together.

The animal's role is one of support and comfort. In rare individuals of exemplary character, they are subjected to horrendous mistreatment, and survive the ordeal so that they may teach humans about fortitude and forgiveness. These unique beings are shining examples of personal sacrifice for the greater good.

If you have an advanced teacher in your life, treat him with the utmost respect and kindness. He is devoting his life to you that you may learn your lessons. The next time your pet presents you with his toy, stop what you are doing and enjoy a game of toss. He is helping you enjoy life, breaking you out of your overthinking. He is showing you how to live.

Look to these wise and free-spirited teachers for guidance. As you examine the choices you have made, remember this… you must not entertain guilt. This emotion is not what you think. If you feel badly about mistreating another, you are inclined to mull it over but do nothing more. We point to your Catholic Church and its confession ritual as an example. A priest dispenses minor punishment and then absolves you of your sin. Guilt is the exchange.

Let us try something new. The next time you feel badly about something you have done, stop and ask yourself what it is about this behavior that attracts you. Look at the act and acknowledge your participation in it. If it brings harm, how can you replace it with something else? Do not rush the process of finding a solution. If you decide to continue the activity, then accept its presence in your life and cease the continuous tapes on self-criticism.

We have given you ideas and information to help you form better relationships with the animals who share your planet. Set aside time to digest our words. Have no judgment. Small steps are advised, as there is much to repair. Be gentle with yourselves, and allow guilt to fade from your memory. This ensures greater understanding and honoring of the Laws of Love.

Chapter 6:
Effective Prayer

*W*e are delighted to bring clarity to yet another misunderstood subject for discussion. Prayer has caused much frustration and disappointment for you. We are here to help you finally make sense of it. Humans have long since thought of prayer as pleading... a request made in earnest for something you want and do not yet possess.

The traditional view and accepted format is as follows: you present your case, hoping your words find favor and touch your Father's Heart. All the while, you are filled with doubt. You worry and think, *"God is too busy to listen. My prayer is not as urgent as some other prayers."* For the more ambitious seekers of redemption, you look for ways to give your prayer greater importance to move it up the list. You say, *"I have been good, Father. Hear my prayer first!"*

You imagine your Heavenly Father is like your earthly father... giving his approval when he is in an agreeable mood, and other times growing impatient and dismissing you. On certain occasions, he answers with a conditional response. If you complete a specific task, for instance, bring home high marks, or trim the grass, then you will earn his praise, and your wish will be granted. Prayer has become, for the most part, a bargaining chip… something to maneuver about the game board… a last resort when all else fails.

Every tactic imaginable has been tried. You have kept detailed records, and there is much inequity, as you have discovered. Those whose prayers were answered did not fit a particular mold. Good people, as you see it, have been denied while those you deem less deserving have been favored. And so you continue to simmer with mistrust while you search for the answers.

When a loved one falls ill, you pray for his return to health. If your prayers fail to produce the desired result, you feel slighted, and you become angry. Some of you more sensitive souls turn your disappointment inward. You feel unimportant in God's eyes. You believe that if He truly loved you, your prayer would be answered. This is your pervading inner turmoil and misperception. For those humans of a more vocal persuasion, you curse your Father and turn your back on Him. You vow to never again believe in His Goodness.

Your heart breaks as you watch your loved one wither away. And when he dies, you decide prayer is useless. You ask, *"How can a loving God allow such a thing?"* You close the door to your heart and throw your prayer books against the wall in anger. You grow cynical about the value of prayer, and some of you denounce your faith. You no longer see the point in it. Why should you sacrifice and work so hard to be a good person if there is nothing in it for you?

This is the state you are in at present. We will help you now to understand prayer, Dear Ones. Be patient as you listen to our words for again, the concept is deep. Here is how it works:

The purpose of prayer is to calm the mind… to bring clarity and peace to better understand what lies beneath and has already been decided. You cannot control the outcome of a decision made by your brother. The only power to live or lay the body down is held by the soul whose life it is. You can say not one thing to change the decision if that soul has determined it is time to retire the form. Oh my, we have given you something you were not expecting.

When a solution to the problem is found, you say, *"Alas, my prayers have been answered!"* But truly, it was already decided… already answered before you asked, and not because you were worthy in God's eyes. All God's Children are worthy! That is why He wishes for nothing but your profound joy in all things. He does not punish you for wrongdoing. It is you who punishes yourselves. The thing that is difficult to comprehend is that the soul's decisions are not made obvious to the Conscious Mind.

This analogy should be of some assistance. A small child rides in the backseat of a car and tries to peer out the window. But his perspective is too low, so he asks, *"Where are we going?"* His loving mother knows exactly where they are going. The child, young and impatient, persists with his questioning. The parent is wise and answers her child in a calm voice. Her words are gentle, carefully chosen so that he can understand. The adult in this story is the soul and the child is the ego self… and the car ride is the life you are currently living. We will give you an example to better illustrate our point.

When a human is nearing the end of a life, he is often filled with fear. This is due to his misconceptions about death and a lack of practical understanding of Eternal Life. The human tries everything to fight the situation, seeking counsel and perhaps employing surgical means. Finally, when all avenues have been exhausted, those in charge of his care say, *"It is time. Let the family come say their good-byes."*

The loved ones file into the room. The family is solemn and woeful… their eyes filled with tears. But in the last hours, something unusual happens. You begin to see a softening of expression on your loved one's face. He has surrendered the ego and allowed Spirit to provide a glimpse of the beauty of what lies beyond the illusion.

It is astonishing to those who remain behind – the peace that comes over these souls. They are seeing from a Higher Perspective. For most humans, it is the first time they have allowed fear to leave them. Whatever pain they have endured, no matter how severe, it is all worth it at that illustrious moment. For there is nothing so precious, so magnificent as the laying down of the heavy burden that is the ego.

This will help you. Try to clear the mind of all preset beliefs. We know this is difficult for you. But it is a required step if you wish to fully assimilate the proper use of prayer.

For a moment, be a child with no memory of prayer whatsoever. You are with your father and mother as you observe them begin to pray. Your parents are kneeling with eyes closed. There is a candle aglow and a pleasant fragrance in the room. You sit on the floor beside them as they begin to speak.

Lord, help us to understand the purpose of this event. Help us to have faith and remember that all things have purpose. We send love and healing to this beloved soul, as we join with our brothers and sisters in bringing Light and Love to those in need. Use me, oh Lord. This is your Body and your Mind. I am here to serve You. May I never forget that. It brings me joy! God, thank you for this glorious life. I am grateful and truly blessed. Amen.

This is an example of a healthy and useful prayer. It is based in gratitude. It is an affirmation of truth. Prayer can also include emotional sentiments and even a venting of frustration. Some religious texts say otherwise. But we can assure you, God does not require of you obedience born out of fear. He is a loving Father, and a loving father-mother is patient, having no issue when a child comes to him with a complaint. In fact, a good parent invites honesty and airing of grievances. Only ego would have a problem with it, and your Father in Heaven is not human. Remember that ego does not exist beyond the world of form.

You may ask, *"What about the time when a life was saved by a surgical operation or a miracle drug?"* Hear us when we say, the decision to continue the life was already made prior to the event that appeared to spare him. Otherwise, all remedies would have the same affect on each and every individual who enlisted them. But humans are not machines punched out on an assembly line. They are Spirit.

An automobile will respond the same way each time fuel is poured into the tank. It will run, no question, as long as nothing else is lacking. But how many different responses could a human have if the body is out of balance and a remedy is used? Your medical journals are filled with thousands of such documented tests and trials, with little if any consensus. The body is in direct communication with the mind at all times, working to complete the soul's lessons in the life. The soul directs the mind and body to help it achieve its goals in completing the curriculum.

You may ask, *"Must I continue the healing protocols? Why should I take any steps to recover if my powerful mind has already decreed it?"* We would applaud such a question, as it shows advanced intellect. The answer is yes, you must… until you retrain the mind. The world of matter still exists, and you are deeply immersed in it. Until you are able to free yourself of its entanglements, go along with the program. Sleep soundly, knowing that in time, you will awaken from the dream and move beyond the world of limitation.

Do you recall our remarks about the body from Chapter 4? Again we have overlaps in the text because all things are connected. There is but one issue… just one problem to solve and that is Love of Self. It is all that is needed to bring healing and peace to any situation. But you do not believe it yet, so we will continue our discussion.

Let us review what prayer is and what it is not. Prayer is not the begging for things or situations to be different than they are. Prayer is not granted nor denied according to a mood. It is not a feeling… it is Law. Prayer is a process of acceptance. God does not need your prayers. You pray and give gratitude for *you*. Any act of praying is done for the sole purpose and benefit of humans. *You* are the ones in need of prayer. It centers you and reminds you of your eternal nature and inheritance.

Praying is a declaration of your connection to God. That is why you engage in prayer, and that is the proper and correct use of it… to help you remember your sacred birthright. A soul in prayer is free from the illusion of fear and doubt. The more time you spend in prayer, the deeper your devotion and the stronger your Faith. You cultivate a greater Love of Self. When you pray for a loved one, you proclaim his perfection as a Child of God. You remind both of you that nothing in the world can take away the essence of who you are.

You do not need permission to send love to any being. If your heart is pure, then your intention is to lift your brother out of darkness. However, when you pray for a result that serves ego or selfishness, then your prayer is no longer coming from light. It must be dropped at once.

If your desire is to reverse a disease, your prayer is akin to skipping a most essential lesson. Nor is it respectful because the soul has chosen the condition to help with his studies. Make sure you understand these parameters. We add this… know that pain can be a powerful motivator.

Here is a fine case in point. A busy executive has little time for the things he sees as minor details, like prayer, or helping the blind, the hungry, or a child in need. He is too busy amassing his fortune. Then his heart gives out and he finds himself in a hospital bed, and suddenly he has time!

You may think he needs a prayer to save him. But he has already been saved. The soul directed the body to assist in the lesson by bringing the heart to a halt momentarily… to reestablish balance and open the heart. Yes, literally in some cases. Remember that a malady in the body correlates to a malady in the mind. The place of any distention and weakness is no mere coincidence.

Do you understand now how futile it is to wish for a different outcome when all is perfectly orchestrated by the wisdom of the body working with the soul? In fact, if your wish were granted, the executive would jump right up out of bed and hurry back to his job. Would he have learned anything? It is doubtful.

We must instill this for your thorough understanding… illness and other mishaps, accidents, losses of all kinds, disasters, and the like, are not punishment. Many still believe in an angry God who punishes His Children. Most religions are based on this idea, which was wrought out of fear and ignorance. The stories were told over thousands of years and not many have come forward to challenge them.

We urge you to reconsider. It is impossible for a Loving Father to be spiteful or punishing. God was not made in man's image. He does not lose his temper, nor his patience. Anger and judgment are aspects of character belonging to ego… and the ego read the scripture incorrectly.

We offer this bit of wisdom for you eager students. There is no power greater than the power of prayer. When two or more souls join together, they can move mountains. Never doubt it. When your loved one is facing death, pray together for his clarity and peace. Affirm his perfection and strength. Remember to state that he is free to move on to the next phase of his learning as he sees fit. If you are not ready to hear it, then pray for *your* acceptance of the situation and your peace of mind.

It is essential that you understand this: it is hurtful to attempt to hold back a soul once he has completed his studies. You must release him. When you plead with him to stay beyond the fulfillment of purpose in a particular lifetime, you prevent both of you from advancing. Know that your relationship does not end with the death of the body. Learn to communicate without it. The absence of form has no power to break your bond or obstruct your connection.

We add this final note. Prayer is also affirming what you are and asking for assistance in receiving. So if you are ready to make a change in vocation for instance, speak of what you envision for a better fit… some directional change, which will allow for more light and greater joy. Then be clear that the job opportunity may present itself in an unexpected way. It may not look as you pictured. Call on us, Dear Ones. We are here to clear up every misunderstanding.

Chapter 7:
Life Purpose

*A*s you begin to grow tired of ego's innumerable distractions and dead ends, you start to look for greater meaning in the world. You begin to appreciate the simpler things, like the sweet smell of honeysuckle carried on the wind or the eucalyptus trees after it rains. Your search has brought you to a clearing and you find yourself asking, *"What is my purpose here?"*

It is at this juncture that you may take up a hobby like bird watching, gardening, or woodworking... or you may volunteer at a homeless shelter. You find yourself looking into the faces of people you have never met. There is warm connection and an unexpected sense of family. You complete the tasks and feel satisfied with how you spent your day. Then you come home and the ego says, *"That can't be my life's purpose."* But this is exactly what you ought to be doing. Do you think the work has no value because it does not pay? Ah, that is your conditioning, Dear Ones. Let it go.

The gift of your time has merit, we can assure you. Your ego is bound to throw a fit. It will say, *"But you didn't really do anything. What about our list of chores and criteria for what is*

valuable? This time spent with strangers does not fit into any category."
Now you can relax knowing you are on the right track.

Your life purpose is to let go of the world you have made, and find your way back to the Self. There is no better way to accomplish this than to be still. Allow Spirit to direct you. Silence the ego's chatter and state your intent to serve. That is your purpose. It is the longing you feel in your gut. Do you doubt our statement? Here is a test to prove our theory...

How satisfied do you feel at your present job? We will give you a hint: if you were fulfilled and joyful, you would not need to read this chapter. So we encourage you to be honest. How joyful do you feel when your day is through? Are you disappointed that you must retire for the evening, and you cannot wait to return in the morning?.. arriving early and eager, face glowing with anticipation? We imagine this is not your answer.

We believe you probably are less than excited to start your day, dragging yourself out of bed, taking as long as possible to get ready, arriving late perhaps, if you can get away with it. You might invent a story to avoid a day's work when you can... when the job becomes too much to bear. But you do not see a way out of your predicament. So you keep going until the body provides your *get-out-of-jail-free* card. We are revisiting the same subject of how the body is commissioned to help with your life lessons.

Here is a scenario you can relate to. You have worked for the same company for 25 years… sat in the same chair, completed the same tasks. And each day, a small voice inside says, *"Please let us do something interesting today. Let us leave here never to return."* But you ignore it. Until one day the chair breaks. You stare for a moment like a caged animal whose door has just been opened. Then you put on the face of disappointment, promising to return upon its repair, as you quickly take your leave.

In the brief time you are away from the desk, you begin to awaken. The mundane tasks that are your work become clear now in your mind. You are now fully aware of the emptiness in your workday. You discover you cannot go back… and that is the best day of your life.

Let us make sure we are in sync. Finding your life purpose is about letting go and rediscovering your joy. What is it that you love to do? Is it music?.. Or do you prefer to dance? Perhaps you have always wanted to teach, or travel on foot, packing only a bedroll and matches to make a fire. But you say, *"How is this serving God or my fellow man?"* We answer you in this manner. What you love to do brings such happiness that you cannot help but share your joy with the world. That inspiration is what your brothers need most.

Humans are happiest in the act of creative expression. Give them something rote and mundane, and they lose their minds. But allow them to sing, dance, and engage in make-believe, and they become as children… full of life and jubilation. You must drop the programming that claims there is a box for this and everything in its place. These are stipulations set forth by a stern schoolmaster who knew nothing of life purpose as creative expression. We return to our discussion with this fine example.

Let us say you are a salesperson. You sell something that holds no meaning for you, except for the paycheck it earns. So now look at what you *do* love about the work. Your specific skill lies in verbal communication. You are adept at convincing others to buy your product. You can talk an Eskimo into purchasing a block of ice from you, or a beachcomber into taking a bag or two of sand. Now let us take this ability and give it new life.

What gives you joy and brings you satisfaction? What do you dream of before attaching the heavy baggage of "someday" to your plans? Perhaps you love the sea. You have taken a boat trip and observed the playful dolphins jump to heights just for the sheer joy of it and their own amusement. Now take your love of speaking and marry it with your love of the sea. What vocation can you imagine would come of this union? Why not create a company where busy office workers can escape from their stressful day to hop aboard your vessel and take a mini cruise around the harbor with you as their captain and tour guide?

Before your ego shoots down the idea, give it time to occupy your thoughts. Explore the possibilities. For the man who loves the sea and enjoys his gift of gab, this is his life purpose. Do you see? It isn't something far off and elusive. Again, that is ego working diligently to make sure you never obtain your goals. Learn to recognize it and you will begin to tune it out... and that will be cause for celebration!

Remember that your life's purpose does not necessarily mean you create a business of your own. There are others like you whom are searching for something meaningful... their place in the Sun. Here is what we suggest: begin to explore your surroundings. If you plan to remain in your city, what is the topography? What does the layout of the land offer and what is its potential?

Nature holds much wisdom and many secrets, so speak to her. Tell her your dreams and ask for guidance. Begin by taking a walk in nature. Be observant. Ideas will come easily to those who sit quietly and listen. Unplug your electronics. Do not take them with you as they will distract and prevent clear communication. Be on the lookout for fellow seekers of truth and purpose. Greet them and be mindful that you may hear something in the conversation that is intended just for you.

Know that when you ask for help, the answer may come in a peculiar fashion. It may be delivered by an animal. We realize that most humans are unaccustomed to speaking with members of the Animal Kingdom. But this again is your perception... more accurately, your *mis*perception, because most of you already speak with animals. There is a canine or feline in nearly every household. They are capable of far more than companionship.

We have given you some ideas to ponder. As we have said many times before, do not rush the process. The important thing to keep in mind is that wisdom requires undoing of present beliefs and mindset. It is not about piling on knowledge or adding to the fact base, but rather a clearing out of what no longer serves.

Here is a simple exercise for you to try. The next time you purchase a book, hold it in your hands and ask for the critical knowledge to come forward. Place the book next to your pillow and repeat the exercise for two or more consecutive nights. Hold the book and announce that only what is truly needed be willing to make itself known. Open the mind for its acceptance. This is a marvelous way to absorb information, and you Dear Children, are capable of it.

We forewarn you not to become too attached to books of facts as they block your own innate power to think and create, and to master your ability. Any time you rely on instructions to guide you, you are no longer thinking for yourself. You have encountered this phenomenon before. We will remind you…

Before the invention of navigational gadgets, you found your way around quite well. You relied on your mind and knew how to read maps or the stars. Some of you navigated with the help of familiar landmarks. But once you began using magnetic trackers, you stopped the flow of input and processing that naturally is available to you from an active thinking mind. You rewired the synapses and bypassed the signals, creating a detour in the brain pattern. Once the signals were ignored for a time, the brain stopped sending them. And now you cannot find your way out of a paper bag without your navigational devices. Ah, it's quite fun to see your world from our vantage point. We implore you to try it.

Would you like to know how it is done? We are happy to tell you. Be still and quiet the mind. Now breathe deeply; close your eyes. Make sure there are no distractions. In your mind's eye, see an expanse of desert. The ground is hot and burns your feet. There is not one green thing, and no water to quench your thirst. You are alone… not even a rodent to keep you company. You look for a drop of water, but there is only a dry riverbed. Hunger gnaws at your belly. You fall to your knees and ask, *"May I see the truth? Please show me the other side."*

Suddenly, the ground beneath you begins to moisten, and little patches of grass sprout up by your feet. In a breath, your world transforms, right before your eyes. A lush and plentiful green valley appears, with a babbling brook, teeming with life. Flowers in vivid shades of violet, pink, and gold cover the valley floor. Birds, frogs, fish, and otters are plentiful as you take in the beauty all around you. You see deer, badgers, and beavers… a fox, and two black bear cubs with their mother. The water sparkles and you recognize a beautiful scent in the air, though you cannot name it.

As you take in the beauty of this special place, you come to a surprising realization. There is a peace here that does not exist in the world you know. You look around to see the animals enjoying their individual activities… foraging, swimming, relaxing… frolicking, parenting, and building nests and burrows. All of these creatures, living in harmony with one another.

You wonder if this is what Heaven looks like. As you gaze at this pristine paradise, you begin to see how easily you can shift the image from one reality to the other. With little effort, you are able to see both worlds. The alarm bell rings and you open your eyes to the desolate dustbowl that is your life… feet dry and cracked, parched lips desperate for a thimble of water. Now manipulate the image and bring a waterfall into the desert. Did you observe how pliable the illusion is now? What you thought was unchangeable is now like a lucid dream.

Keep flipping the images in your mind… from the bleak desert to the lush meadow or snowy mountain peak or tropical island. Continue working with this until you are able to envision the land of plenty – God's Kingdom of Heaven. Now you have one foot in both worlds. Fear can no longer hold you hostage. And you will never again feel alone.

We will sum up this section by reminding you that the world you think is so solid and permanent is nothing of the sort. It is ever changing… and it is changing according to your belief. That is the remarkable aspect that drives all you see. This is why we aim to help you awaken from your slumber. The more of you humans that come to your senses, the greater the power you have to dispel fear and doubt. There is a glorious and perfect place, just waiting for your discovery. When you are ready, take a leap forward!

Begin by seeing the edges of illusion. You can do this. The next time someone invites you to join in their unhappy game, politely excuse yourself and do not engage in it. Whether it is gossip or watching a violent film, or participating in any act that harms the body or mind. If it is your normal practice, allow for something greater to take its place.

There is a misconception among humans. You believe it takes great effort and discipline to accomplish the higher tasks that we speak of, as described in the Holy Bible. But hear us now. The only thing required of you is your willingness to see a thing differently.

This is a great truth. It must be written down and kept at your bedside. Be willing to see an event or situation in a different light and you will be free of its hold on you. And that begins the healing process. What a gem you now have in your possession!

We now conclude this chapter by suggesting that you start small in finding something that truly interests you, and begin to incorporate it into your daily routine. Just allow for the possibility that life can be a joy… because it can and should be, Dear Ones. Free yourselves of the heaviness of wrangling your life's purpose like roping a steer. It is not that difficult, we assure you. Just take one day at a time. This is sound advice. Do not spend months planning. Just begin. Start somewhere and make adjustments as needed.

One last thought. Give yourself fully to the task at hand. Whatever you have agreed to… whether it is time spent with a friend or working at your present job that you do not love. Be fully present. This is not a catch phrase. It is a commandment, and it will serve you well to obey it.

Be joyful even when you are performing the tasks you do not relish, because you now understand how easily the illusion can shift. The dusty desert is a mere façade. Remember what you have seen in your mind and never forget the truth of that vision. When your belly aches, enjoy the cool breezes and fruit-filled orchard. Truly it is your decision. Which world will you choose to live in? It is entirely up to you.

Chapter 8:
The Power of Forgiveness

The idea of forgiveness is not a welcome thought to most humans. It is considered a last resort because the ego never wants to give up the fight. So the obvious question is, why do it? Why go to the trouble of letting someone off the hook for his bad behavior? We will start our discussion with the *why* and then move on to the *how*. Let us look at what you currently do when a brother does something hurtful.

The first thing you humans do is retaliate. An eye for an eye, as the saying goes. *"You cut off my arm and now I will cut off yours. You took my spouse and I will now take yours."* Of course one retaliatory act is followed by another and the cycle never ends. This is what your world looks like. Tribe fights against tribe, nation pitted against nation, on every continent throughout the world. There is no end in sight… no final blow, because it merely invites the next. *The war to end all wars* is a game you play with yourselves. It cannot possibly solve the problem and you know this. It keeps the fight alive. And how well has that served you?

How joyful does it make the Sons and Daughters of God to fight with one another? You refuse to lay down your weapon for fear that if you do, your enemy will seize that moment to draw his sword and pierce you through the heart with it. So even when you have agreed upon a ceasefire, you keep your weapon ready at your side. Again we ask you... how content are you with this practice? Are you willing to consider another approach?

If you are open to the idea, we will begin. Start small. Choose someone with whom you have only a minor disagreement. Let us say he misrepresented an item for purchase. Your brother came to your house and offered to sell you a cleaning product. He demonstrated its impressive cleaning power and you said, *"I will take one, please."* Then he took your money and slipped away... and as you examined your purchase, you discovered it was not as promised. You ran out the door to confront him, but he was nowhere to be found. Now, how should you handle this?

"He is a thief!" you cry. You tell everyone in town how he cheated you. But every time you tell the tale, it only makes you angrier. The retelling of the story does not bring healing nor peace. It seems you hardly remember what you ate for breakfast, but you can recall every minute detail of your brief encounter with this brother, for all the remainder of your days on earth. The stories grow old and you have become bored with the sound of your own voice. So let us try something new.

For the purpose of this exercise, we shall name this brother *John*. We shall begin the same way we have instructed you throughout this book. Be still and close your eyes. Have no distractions. Take a deep breath and exhale slowly. Now speak to John. Ask him to attend a hearing… an airing of grievances. This will be done in the mind. The ego will be working furiously to sabotage your meeting. Beware of this and do not allow it.

Now John has appeared. Let him in and ask him to sit down. Begin to describe what he did to bring you harm. Spare no detail. You must be honest about how his actions affected you. Do not rush this very important step in the forgiveness process. Once you have said all, be still. Sit quietly and invite John to respond. This will undoubtedly be challenging for you. But remember that no harm can come to you in this environment of genuine intent and desire to repair the rift between you.

Listen intently to what your brother has to say. There is much to be expressed, for you each have your point of view and each of you sees the event as only he can.

While John is speaking, you notice that he has a quiver in his voice. He is not strong, and you did not see that before. Your anger has subsided. So you begin to truly look at him for the first time since your initial meeting. You see his tattered shirt and glance down at his faded trousers. His shoes are scuffed. He has no wedding ring, and you suddenly realize he has walked a great distance to come to your home.

You begin to see John in a new light. He is not proud of his behavior nor is he able to look you in the eye. You recognize his shame, and you feel a sense of sadness. There is silence… John wants your forgiveness. He is in pain. For no Child of God mistreats a brother if he is wholly loved and at peace with himself.

It is impossible to do harm outwardly without the prerequisite of personal suffering. The outer reflects the inner. Do you see? The disease must exist inside the body-mind first, before ego begins looking for an outlet, a place to engage and express rage. It is the way pain is dealt with… an out-picturing of what is left unfinished and unresolved. The soul signs up for the class to learn the lesson. The life pattern you see repeating over and over is simply a continuation of a class that may take years or perhaps several lifetimes to complete.

We now move forward to help heal this dear wounded brother. Take his hand and look into his woeful eyes. Tell him you forgive his misstep, and watch as his face lightens. The furled brow eases; he manages a smile. That is his way of saying, *"thank you."* He is showing gratitude to you for giving him the gift of your acceptance and love. Do you realize that is why you came together in the first place?.. to work through his pain and yours too?

Remember what we have told you – that all events have purpose. Now we can conclude our session. Thank John for coming to your mind and listening to your words. There is now peace between you. You will never again have consternation with this brother. Now take what you have learned and apply it to yet another circumstance… this next one considerably more challenging.

You were just a boy of eight. You were fishing at the end of a pier with your friend, whom we will name, *Thomas.* Without warning, he struck you and you fell in the river. He moved away soon after and to this day, you are frightened of the water. You remember the feeling of being helpless and that is what haunts you most. You have repeated a pattern of needing to be in control of all the details of your life. Your spouse is obedient, as are your children. You allow no one to enter what you consider your safe space.

Thomas has left his mark on you. Would you like to make peace with this brother? You reply, *"Of course not! He doesn't deserve my forgiveness."* But we ask you this… what has been the price tag for this hostility? You are unable to enjoy so many moments of your life. You are carrying a heavy load, Dear Human. Would you not like to be free of it?

We will guide you. In very similar fashion as your session with John, invite Thomas into your mind. You must now speak. Say everything to this brother. Hold nothing back. *"How could you try to kill me?"* you cry. *"There is no excuse for what you have done. You are evil and I will never forgive you!"* you shout. You have not ever spoken these words before, and they pierce your own eardrums as you say them. You are allowed to express in this way. It is a definable, pragmatic solution, and the only true means for clearing.

Purging in this manner is exhausting, yet much needed and vital to the process, just as the purging of poisons held in the body. For that is exactly what hate creates… a chemical reaction in the tissues. It is corrosive, transforming healthy blood and organs into cancerous cells that must be expelled at once.

You look into Thomas's face. You have not done so since the incident. And as you do so, you realize he is not the monster you thought. He is human… a Child of God just as you are. *"But why did he do it?"* you ask. *"Why pick on me? He is a bully!"* We will tell you.

The home he grew up in was a broken one, full of fighting. Someone was always throwing something against a wall… a china plate, family photos, or the loving wife. The parental figure with a short fuse created a frightening home life of which your friend Thomas was exposed to daily. He never told you; he was too proud. So he kept it inside, and one day, as you looked especially dapper in your birthday shirt and whistling a happy tune, he became enraged with jealousy and aimed to harm you… to squeeze the life out of you in order to ease his pain.

We tell you truly, no Child of God can do harm to another soul without pain in his heart. We repeat this to ensure that you understand and remember it when your brother attempts to hurt you. Instead of reacting in fear – and that is what anger is, fear disguised – just be still. Allow him to deliver his punch. Say nothing at all. Humans are so accustomed to speaking, but much more can be said with no words at all.

Turn the other cheek as you have been instructed in the Holy Book. Try this once and you will see something shift. Give this brother your love in that moment and you will end the altercation instantly. If you wish to continue it, then by all means punch back. Again we say, it is up to you what kind of life and experience you wish to have during your stay on earth.

When you build your towering prison walls, you think you are protecting yourselves. But you have blocked out the sun and all your joy along with it. As a result, you feel despondent; downhearted. So let us help you repair it. Begin small. Think of a minor incident… a trivial quarrel involving a brother whom you have refused to forgive. Start there and follow the steps. Begin speaking to him, allowing your emotions to surface. Do not be afraid of them. They serve you well.

We give you this next example to further demonstrate the merits of forgiveness. Think back to a time when you had a fierce disagreement with someone you hardly knew. Nothing he said made any sense to you, and he felt the same way about you. Your mutual hostility toward one another was the only thing you could agree upon. You each wanted nothing more to do with the other. In fact if you could have arranged it, you would have removed him from your life altogether, banishing him to another world.

But as luck would have it, you were forced to share a living [or work] space. One day, something unexpected happened. After a heated argument and near clash, there was a noticeable shift... a metamorphosis. You found yourselves in a moment of camaraderie. For the first time, you were in agreement, and you began to laugh. Neither of you knew what happened, but you saw each other in a new light.

Where you once were sworn enemies, you are now dear comrades. This union is stronger than if you had not ever fought. And why is that? If you can answer this question, then you are on your way to becoming peacemakers. They are sorely needed on your planet at this moment in your history. And for those who wish it, we are here to help you achieve this.

Here is your answer. The peace born of that kind of commitment is far more satisfying, and your bond reflects that earnest effort and promise to solve the problem. It is not unlike a solid marriage in which both partners vow to stay in the relationship and work together no matter what they are faced with. Do you see how that draws two souls closer than if they got along famously from the get-go?

If you cannot open the door while your classmate is still standing outside your mind, then ask for help. We will give you a place to start. Speak these words: *Lord, help me to be willing to consider the possibility of forgiving this person someday.* That is your only requirement at this time… just be willing to allow for the possibility of peace between you. Let all else go. Do not concern yourself with the *how* of it. Once your stubbornness gives way, remove the excess words in the phrase until you distill it down to just these two: *I forgive.*

Know that a soul who has left the world of form and returned to Spirit is also in need of healing. All souls need your forgiveness… and you need theirs. Trust us when we say, this is a mutual process even if it does not appear so. If a brother has done great harm, perhaps taken the life of your child, and you see nothing that connects you to him, the exercise holds even greater importance. You summoned him. You asked him to help you with your lesson.

This is the hardest part for humans to comprehend. Your vision is extremely narrow. Without your inclusion of eternal life, you cannot see the lesson, nor your part in it.

If you are not enjoying this life of yours, Dear Ones, then you are not challenging yourselves with anything. The muscles you neglect to exercise will not support you when you eventually need them. So stretch yourselves! Go out on a limb and take chances that require courage. Go ahead and hurt your pride. Be willing to make fools of yourselves and see what comes of it. You will be pleasantly surprised.

We give you one last example. A husband batters his wife, and the town condemns this lost brother for his awful deed. The wife stays for fear of repercussion, caring for the child they made together. As the years pass, the child grows to maturity and moves away. The wife deteriorates and becomes diseased. She dies, and the husband, hearty and robust as ever, lives on. The perception is that there is grave injustice. An innocent woman was beaten to death, literally. And the husband got away with murder. How could anyone forgive such a horrendous thing?

Here is the answer. These two souls joined to learn a life lesson together. He learns about the pain and remorse of harming an innocent being. And she learns about the damage one causes to Self when allowing another to mistreat her. She does not speak up and that is her sin. His sin is hitting and her sin is allowing it. Do you see? So if she begins to speak up, he then has a decision to make. He will either move past the abusive behavior, or he will continue as before and seek another classmate [recipient].

You ask, *"How is that fair? He will just hurt another innocent victim."* Yes, he will. And yes, it is fair because the next "victim" will need the lesson too. He is serving a purpose by playing the role. This is not an easy concept. Your job is to bring justice to inequity… not by locking up criminals but by listening to these souls. When someone is in pain and they lash out, what good does it do to punish them? It is far wiser to hear them out. Yes, they will continue to punch the air for a few minutes more until they learn to trust again.

You may wonder, *"If the battering husband is fulfilling a need by teaching a spiritual lesson, then should he be allowed to roam free as if he has done nothing wrong?"* This is where the answers become more advanced and require greater thought and explanation. The answer is, yes and no. First, you must remember that your world is a world of duality. So the answers are two-fold and one may appear to be in direct opposition to the other. Questions are asked on a level that does not correlate to the reality of your illusion. We must break this down for you…

Begin by knowing that a lost soul needs assistance in finding his way back. So it would be careless to let a murderer roam the streets. As long as there is intent to harm, then it is irresponsible to allow him to continue marauding.

We remind you that all souls are Children of God. They are deserving of love and kindness, regardless of what they have done in the eyes of the law. God is the only Law that is truly valid. So the answer is, give these brothers a safe place in which to express their frustration and begin to heal.

For some of them, they may always require a special home, away from the typical triggers. Look at these particular cases just as you would any other wounded being. An eagle whose wing has been permanently damaged cannot soar to the heights he once could. He cannot fend for himself. So he spends the remainder of his days in a sanctuary. His life is made enjoyable enough, despite his disability.

As you can see, there is much to unlearn and correct before your world is at peace. We are here to help. Begin with this one small task. Bring a person into the mind and heal the rift between you. That is your assignment. If you are not exactly sure if you agree with anything we have said, take our challenge and try the exercise regardless. Then if you do not see the point in it, you are free to continue your fighting and building your tall towers lined with armed guards.

It will be interesting to see how this story plays out, especially if a great number of you engage in what we have proposed. It will be a new world, and we believe you are ready for it. Bless you, Dear Ones. It is a very exciting time for the inhabitants of your planet.

Chapter 9:
The Tapestry

*F*or the remainder of this guidebook, we will address some of your most pressing questions. We will be covering several subjects, one leading into another. We have already spoken about your need to know who you are and why you are here, and the pointlessness of following the ego's advice. But let us now augment what we have stated with the following...

Humans possess a highly functioning brain. It never sleeps as you know, and it is always searching for answers. This serves you well, for the most part. It can also get in the way because the constant questioning is like a toddler who cannot stop his inquiries long enough to hear the answer to his own question. Silence is the key that opens the door to wisdom, so you must learn to quiet the mind. This is where discipline will serve you well. Allow your mind to question without feeling obliged to reply. Let it be frustrated for a time and it will find something new to occupy it.

We would now like to bring an important point to your attention, though we have mentioned it before. Greed is a disease, Dear Ones. Your ego has already instructed you to skip over this section and you are nearly convinced to do so.

But take a breath and hear us when we say, the lack of joy and peace in your lives is due to the pursuit of great fortune without a solid foundation beneath you.

For those of you who lose your balance and are unable to regain your equilibrium, this section is for you. If you are positive that we are not speaking to you, read on. Here is a test. Can you imagine giving away all you possess and still being happy in the world? Now you know for certain if this passage is meant for you. This is the answer to the prayer you did not know you prayed. Let us explain…

You pursue the almighty dollar, hardly able to focus on anything else. You believe money is your lifeline because the world has convinced you of it. Everything you buy and value is attached to it. We remind you, only one hundred years ago, townsfolk traded their wares. It was not a chore but a joyful exchange on many levels. Its social aspects were a draw and keenly appreciated. So the past century has completely upended your way of life. Now you cannot live without your purchases and the paper that holds no value.

You dispense with all else to obtain your wealth. Relationships fall by the wayside and children grow up without your being there to witness it. And one day, a young man interrupts while you are counting your money and says, *"I'm leaving."* You look up from your stack of currency, puzzled as you try to decipher what he said. This figure before you with bags packed looks familiar. Suddenly you realize he is your adult son. You ask, "*But when did you grow to be so tall? You were just a child ten minutes ago.*"

You would like to think this is a fabrication or that it does not happen often, but you know the truth. The greatest problem as we see it is not finding your way back to meaningful work and connected relationships. The greatest obstacle is your disbelief that it can be done and that it is worth the effort. We now give you the answer and ask you to test our theory for yourself.

Humans are inclined to take a shortcut when they can find one. That is because the prize has become more important than the path that leads you… the end taking precedence over the means. It is especially evident pertaining to monetary wealth, but it has spread to all other areas of your human life. We encourage you to rethink this, Dear Ones. The value of relationships has also been drastically diminished as a result of pushing ahead in careless fashion. We will demonstrate.

The reward is a moment of heartfelt connection… a physical coupling in which the one you love looks deeply into your eyes and says those words you long to hear and yet are so deathly afraid of. Humans desire this moment of loving connection more than anything else in the world. Your lust for money, mind-altering substances, or any other thing is actually a yearning for love between two souls. You know this, but you pretend to desire something else because the other objects of your affection cannot break your heart.

So you chase the dollar bill or food or drug and it says, "*Of course, I love you.*" And then you are satisfied for a moment.

But it is fleeting. Now you must have more. You are fixated on that thing, which you have chosen to replace God's Love. So you work twice as hard to satisfy that craving, but the thrill has begun to wane. In the final stage, you have mutated into someone you no longer recognize… crawling along the floor begging for still more of whatever you have now become addicted to until someone steps in to rescue you.

Greed, fear, or addiction… it is all the same. The paths you have chosen lead nowhere and that is your predicament. You must reconnect with your true nature, which is to create. You have forgotten the joy and satisfaction that come from building things… to take an empty space and fill it with something of your own design. Do you recall your childhood and the various games you played? As you matured, you allowed a system to infiltrate and crush your creative tendencies. But that is not who you are. It is time to reengage the imagination.

We have a solution for you. Choose a spot and build something modest. Construct a critter box or a child's fortress, bake a pie from scratch, or splatter paint on a canvas. Perhaps you will take on something more ambitious like designing a waterfall or building a home of earth. Some of you may think of this as manual labor — time wasted and beneath you. So you slave over your computer screen instead, eyes glazed over, until you cannot remember your own moniker. Are you not willing to explore other avenues? Put aside just one hour and follow our suggestion. But in that hour, give it your full attention. Then you can decide what holds value for you.

Let us now take this idea to the next level. The relationship you build from scratch is far more rewarding than the prearranged matching of which you have no emotional investment. So take your time to create a life together instead of engaging in a brief encounter. The use of shortcuts in relationships produces feelings of emptiness and guilt. The moment of excitement quickly passes and then you lose interest and move on.

Have you no memory of the chills of anticipation born of longing and a strong current of familiarity? Of course you remember it, for you speak of this first love as if it were yesterday. You must do as you did then… allow the flower petals of your love to open naturally. If you attempt to force the bud open, the result is death to the rose, and the destruction of your love.

Skipping important steps causes a human to be thrown off kilter. That leads to addiction, as we mentioned earlier. Can you not see the similarities between the drug addict, the glutton, and all other imbalanced pursuits? We are focusing on the aspects of blinded vision and the shutting out of human connection. This applies to so many areas of your lackluster lives. You must keep your feet on solid ground.

That is what your Father meant when He said, "Seek ye first the Kingdom of Heaven." The first Commandment, to have no other gods before the Lord, is first for a reason. Read these words without judgment, Dear Ones, and you will find the pearl.

Knowing who you are and why you have all come helps to plant one's feet. Then you can grow anything in God's Garden without worry of overgrowth by weeds. Do you understand the metaphor? You need not be concerned about an endeavor taking a wrong turn, as you no longer need the lesson that would correct the misstep.

We can now revisit your beliefs as they relate to wealth and greed. Greed is a perfect example of a wrong turn… a detour of oftentimes exceptional magnitude. If one possesses nothing but the clothes upon his back but he has enough to give to others less fortunate, then he is the rich man. While the millionaire who cries about his dwindling investment interest is the poor man, for he is in constant fear of losing his money. We urge you to take stock of your beliefs regarding prosperity. This manual is not intended to stifle, imprison, or cause guilt. Its purpose is to open the mind and promote change.

This observation should be helpful as we introduce a new subject for you to ponder. Your world is continually focusing on appearances. What a man is wearing, his coifed hair or the shine upon his polished dress shoes is of little value. But you have made it into a calling card. You are not looking at his character or anything else of value… just what he has adorned the body with. We encourage you now to retrain the eyes to look past the façade.

We invite you to try an experiment. Set aside your comb and typical grooming routine for the moment. Dress in your oldest rags and take to the streets where you will not be recognized. Sit barefoot on the sidewalk and observe the passersby. You will find that most look away, paying you no mind at all. They wish nothing to do with you because you represent something they fear. You are penniless, or so they think… and they worry you might steal their wallets. They imagine you have a disease, so they will not shake your hand. This is an eye opening experiment and should be part of a school curriculum. It would open the door to greater understanding and a breaking down of pre-held beliefs.

The many prejudices humans hold must be addressed now, as they can no longer persist. The belief system that held them in place was built on lies. It has begun to crumble, and that is a good thing. You know the phrase, *"It is darkest before the dawn."* This refers to the last few holdouts when a major shift is about to take place. It is the child's clothing that he has outgrown but refuses to discard.

It was not long ago that modern civilization in your part of the world thought only those with the lightest of skin were capable of intelligent thought, worthy of an audience. And for the males light of skin, this idea worked well. But the Sons and Daughters of God come in all colors, and not one color nor shape nor size nor status is more deserving than another.

Have you not discovered this? Of course you have. But those in the good seats are unwilling to allow for a new mindset, as it is disruptive to their lives. It is the stadium bench where the businessmen enjoy their spectator game. Along comes a stranger, and the men have to move aside to make room for him. They grumble a bit and then resume their enjoyment of the game.

But soon arrives another newcomer and then another… and the men watch in horror and call an emergency meeting. They exclaim, *"This is <u>our</u> bench… something must be done!"* And so begins the fighting and marking of territory, and eventually a knife is drawn and a man is stabbed to death. This story depicts your history, Dear Ones, and the story is not over. For you are still learning the lesson.

We give you this as a window to allow light into the darkened room. For a moment, judge nothing by reading with an open mind. You are not yet born. You are considering your next adventure, deciding where to live. What part of the world will you choose? You create a basic structure for the lifetime ahead. You have been a king and a beggar, a mother and a tailor, a thief, a priest, and a soldier. You have lived long lives and short. You have been rich and poor, and resided in every part of the world. You weigh your options and decide you will be born in South America and you will be a biologist in your adulthood.

You cast your invitation into the pool of Shared Consciousness, a place where all souls commune and share One Mind. In Spirit, you meet with a young Chilean couple. The husband is large-boned and a fisherman, and the petite wife keeps the home and will raise their children. They accept your invitation to join their family. They are law-abiding people of humble means with lessons, which include diminished sense of self, belief in lack, and dependency. You share many of the same life lessons, and that is why you have chosen them.

Now you know many of the traits and details of your life ahead including your skin and hair color, body type, religion, language, and social status. Do you see where we are headed in this story? If you remain in the village where you were born, then you will be accepted. But what if you venture out to a far off land where you are a stranger? You will not look like the locals, and you find the people there are apt to fear you. If they have been told wild stories about tribesmen from other places, they will not trust you, merely based on your appearance.

Do you now see that judgment of the body is without merit? Know that you chose it. We understand how most of you will react to what we have just told you. But this is not a study guide for youngsters. It is a course in Higher Learning. You would not have this book in your hands if you were not ready for it. So let us repeat the statement and delve further into its meaning.

Each soul chooses a family along with characteristics and the basic parameters… a lesson plan if you will of what will be accomplished in the lifetime. So spending the life cursing your body or anyone else's is ludicrous. In a moment, it will be over, and you will laugh at the silliness of it all. Then you will return to a life of form in a new body, picking up right where you left off.

Let us be clear when we say, those of you who have suffered are more courageous than you ever imagined. Again, we sight the child riding along in the backseat. You cannot remember agreeing to be stolen from your land and put to work as slaves or sent to gas chambers. Many other tribesmen in other lands have also endured horrific, unspeakable things. And yes, they have all agreed to them.

You must understand this one truth that ties in like a golden thread ever so strong: you are all dreaming this dream together. That is why great numbers of you have the same experience… why there are concert halls and sports arenas, tsunamis and earthquakes… great buildings bursting at the seams, communal houses of blended families, plagues, and widespread famine. Hear us when we say, nothing is tragic. It is your decision to view it that way if you so choose. This again is a deep concept, so allow us to explain it further.

Let us consider a group of travelers on a cruise liner. On the surface things appear random and unplanned as the ship begins to head into choppy seas. Then the alarm sounds and the passengers are in a panic as they charge for the lifeboat. After the dust settles, some of the souls have perished. You perceive the event as awful and commence with your investigation to lay blame… to find fault with the captain or crew, the ship's design, or her instruments. You feel badly for the young wife who lost her husband just as you do the child who dies having lived just 7 years. You ask, *"What could possibly be gained from this tragedy? Why do some people have to die young?"*

It must be understood that a short life is no better or worse than a long life. The curriculum is what determines the length of a soul's incarnation. The schoolwork to be completed is the determining factor. It is not an elective, but required. Upon its completion, the soul decides whether to stay and start something else or to leave the body and the life to rest awhile.

Let us discuss the child who dies young. To get a better perspective, it is wise to ask someone who has experienced such a thing. If you ask a parent what kind of life they had with that special being who came into the world with unique circumstances, they will tell you with tears of joy and heartfelt appreciation of how blessed they were to have known that remarkable soul. Their love goes well beyond the pain endured, and they would not trade that brief time for anything on earth.

So Dear Humans, we urge you to try seeing your world through our eyes. It is a wondrous place full of adventure and challenges, miracles and joyful surprises. The human experience is spectacular as witnessed from our vantage point. You must learn to stand with one foot in the illusion and one foot out, as that will offer a much better view.

We wish to discuss one last area of importance as we conclude this chapter. It is the gift of service. We spoke about it briefly, but we will elaborate here because it is so important.

You view service to another being as something reserved for the elderly or those who have servants, leaving them with considerable time on their hands. You say, *"I have no time right now… I am raising a family. I'm too busy to take on charity work."* This is how you see it. Your guilt seeps in and you drag yourselves to church and place a spare bill in the coffers. Then you head home and that is sufficient in your mind. Because the money will go to people dedicated to helping others, so indirectly, you have helped someone. This is your deductive reasoning. Let us offer clarity.

What you are actually doing is sloughing off another essential aspect of your humanity. Have you known anyone who sat in a chair at the highest level, refusing to get his hands dirty? He towers over all. He is disconnected, having no idea what life is like for those around him. He will not sweep the floor nor change a baby's diaper, nor answer his own phone. Why is that so important, you ask? Because

Dear Ones, that is how you reconnect with your brothers…
and with your Self. The emptiness you feel inside comes
from a false sense of superiority. Reconnection fills the
heart with joy. This is the first step to healing the
Separation. It is the obstacle that stands in the way of
everything you desire, though you do not realize it.

If you thought the Separation [between you and your fellow
humans] stood in the way of your next paycheck, you would
do everything in your power to destroy it. If the Separation
were deemed to be a threat to your nation's security, your
government would have it arrested and put to death.

Can you see how your beliefs dictate how you live your
lives? Every judgment you make is rooted in your belief
system. Here is our suggestion. Set aside just one hour every
month for a soul in need. Find something you would enjoy
doing while helping another. Will you try it just once? Then
you can decide if you would like to repeat it.

If you must attach a payoff as you humans are so
accustomed to, then do so. Give yourself a reward once you
have completed the task. But remember that attaching a
reward often kills the joy inherent in the simple act of
giving. What was once an inspired and creative expression
now becomes a chore, and you will look for a reward every
time, thereafter. That is the deep flaw in the reward system.
We suggest that you return to some of the old ways,
including trading of wares. You will find pleasure in it, as

people did for thousands of years. It can be done, even in a modern society.

We have given you a map… some guidelines for how to find your way in the world of form. Now it is up to you. Honor your need for time to think it through. Consider our comments. We have planted seeds, Dear Ones. Give weight to what we have said, and do the simple things we have suggested. Make small changes – small, but not insignificant. Spend less time listening to your ego and more time listening to your Heart.

We are always here for you, Dears Ones. You are the Children of God, and He has proclaimed your worthiness to inherit His Kingdom. Do not shy away from Him. He is your Father who loves you beyond words. You are afraid to love something or someone so much because you fear you will lose your love. The thought is unbearable so you pretend you do not care. But we see everything. Your love has not changed nor has His. Give thanks that the world and all its pain is not real. It is your classroom; a place to visit while you are away from Home.

We tell you it has been an honor to enlighten you on the pages of this guidebook. Know that we take every step with you. That is our assignment for which we are most grateful. We watched you as you took your first steps and we are here now as you begin to see the flaws in the structure that is your waking life. You have made many assumptions about the world you live in. We will give you a heads up…

gravity is not what you think, nor is the simple math equation, *2 + 2 = 4.* Be willing to allow for something much greater.

Let go of *good, bad, right,* and *wrong,* and all your preconceived notions on every subject. You are in the habit of choosing teams, and you do it throughout your day. Will you accept one last assignment? It is quite simple. Just begin to notice how often you take a side during your conversations. Now try listening without judgment, and you will begin to break down the walls that are now too high for even *you* to scale. Let them tumble. Take a deep breath and exhale the last bit of doubt from your mind.

Your world is soon to be reborn… all things to be flooded with Light and made new. The spring is coming after a long, harsh winter. Have faith, Dear Ones. Your Father has not forgotten you. Every one of you is part of His Grand Design. Soon, you will see the long-awaited front side of the Tapestry. It is a glorious masterpiece to behold!

Atlanta Botanical Gardens

What should we do to protect ourselves from terrorists?

You may not be ready for our answer so take it slow and listen without judgment. There is a love-hate relationship that your brothers who live in other countries have for you in America. They watch everything you do. They learn your language, listen to your music, copy your trend-setting fashions and the way you speak, buy your gadgets and stylish sneakers.

They want to be like you, but that also creates animosity and jealousy. So the solution is not as simple as you were hoping. The answer is to embrace them, Dear Ones... not cast them aside and build unscalable walls. You must find ways to include these brothers and help them create the world they covet right where they live. If you ask these countrymen if they prefer to leave or stay in their homelands, most would say they prefer to stay. The one variable is their lack of wealth. So the problem is actually a lack of self love. Your rejection of these souls is not helping to solve the problem.

You are no better than these brothers, though many presume they are. Those readers who have older brothers can relate to our words when they recall feeling inferior next to their sibling. That is the case here. Look past the color of their skin and native tongue and you will see your many similarities. Now take another moment while you consider the things you want for your lives, all of which you have in common.

Now what would you do for your little brother to help him build his self-esteem? Might you give him a hand as he attempts to climb the ladder to join you? You are so fearful of what might happen if you extend kindness to these individuals. But what of the soldiers who have come to unknown regions with a job to do? They met the villagers and befriended them. They soon discovered these people are not the enemy after all. Ignorance, greed, hate… these are your true enemies.

So take it slow and give yourselves sufficient time to comprehend what we have said. Start small as we often suggest. Speak to these brothers in your mind and begin to forgive them for their misguided deeds. Then forgive yourselves for your ignorance, blind obedience, and judgment of people you know nothing of.

Connect with what you have in common and begin to tear down the wall between you. If this is done in the mind and nowhere else, you have accomplished much. Take a second step and begin a conversation with a brother. And the next time you hear rhetoric aimed at furthering the ignorance and fear, do not listen. Allow it to fade, for you no longer believe it.

Our nation is divided since the election. Do you have any suggestions regarding our president?

Yes. First, remember that your elected figurehead is a conglomerate… a cumulated mix of shared thought… the representation of those unexpressed feelings emerging as one body, in the form of one man. It is symbolic more than a specific individual. He represents the materializing of shared frustration and cries of woe in so many areas of your lives. From politics to law enforcement, to social behavior and the school system, interactions between souls at the workplace, and everywhere you engage with your brothers. It is your disappointment and rage, summed up and embodied in one person with a chosen name.

But you are misunderstanding his purpose if you condemn him and lay blame on the soul and body that is your reigning president. If you are unhappy with what he says or does, it is you who must look deeply into your own actions and participation or lack thereof in the decisions that impact you and your brothers, and all inhabitants of your planet. He is not unlike so many chosen targets throughout your history. Some praise and some curse him. He is canonized and criticized. So what can be done to repair the rift… the great divide?

Begin by gathering together in a peaceful manner. All attendees must agree to the rules of respectful meeting of council. You may speak in a calm manner without finger-pointing and no raising of voices. Choose a leader for each side. And there is to be a grand marshal – a head speaker who will remain impartial. Hold your meeting and do not go over the time limit. Permit no unhealthy food or drink, as a clear mind is imperative. If you follow these guidelines, your meeting will render some very usable solutions of which you are to pass along to political heads and leaders on both sides.

You must ignore the titles and categories if you truly wish to solve the problem of division. There is dissention among the ranks. But you are one people, one nation, one Son... the Children of God. Your president is your classmate. He is no lesser than you; no less deserving of love and forgiveness for his missteps of which you are also capable.

Can you imagine how you would respond to the darts and arrows flung in your direction on a daily basis coming from all directions? If you thought you could handle things better, would you not do so? What is stopping you? This soul has a thick skin. Do not be fooled by his crassness or lack of grace. He is no monster. Under the gruff exterior beats a human heart with red blood coursing throughout. This brother is flesh and bone, same as you.

So refrain from your casting of stones. Can you help him with the monumental task at hand? Send him your support and offer your advice. He is listening, as you are already aware. This human has volunteered to steer your vessel through a great storm. But he cannot do it alone. He needs every one of you. Will you act as shipmates or will you declare a mutiny and conspire to sink the ship? What you do next is up to you. So think on it with care, Dear Ones. Your thoughts and words have power. Never forget that.

Why do the rich get richer and the poor get poorer?

The disparagement is growing and so is the animosity at the injustice of it all. Greed is the seed that grew the stubborn weeds that have overtaken the delicate garden. So yes... something must be done. We ask you once again to speak to these individuals in your mind. Tell them of the pain they have caused. While they sit comfortably on their overstuffed cushions of silk, you scrounge on the floor like mice in search of a tidbit leftover from their decadent 5-course meal. It has been set in motion, and inertia now dictates. Control is no longer in the hands of the one who created it. The monster takes on a life of its own.

So how can we put the jack back in his box? It requires a feat of great effort and skill but mostly, of genuine intent to reestablish and restore equality. Do you remember our story about the businessmen on the spectator bench and their unwillingness to share their fine seating with strangers? Well, here we are again revisiting this story because there is but one problem and but one solution to all concerns. Here is what we suggest...

You will be working together, for there is power in numbers. Hold a meeting with open hearts and good intentions. Amass your resources and present your ideas in a forum where someone at the helm will serve as guide. Come up with 3 or 4 good ideas. You will be establishing a partnership of sorts and pooling your monies in order to create a strong presence in your community.

Choose an endeavor of which you can participate fully. You will give of your time, and it will be something that inspires you. Is it a general goods emporium?.. apparel or hardware store?.. or diner? Perhaps a center for learning. Select something that is needed in the community and that also fits your particular talents. Now vow to patronize this place of business that you will build together.

If you have chosen wisely and followed these steps, this new place of business will attract customers from near and far. The initial 5 or so investors, creators of a dream job and purveyors of freedom from poverty, will mushroom into 50 and then 500 workers who enjoy their day's work and are freed from the bonds of destitution and hardship. Do you see how easily it can be solved?

Remember that some individuals only wish to complain and do not intend on solving anything. Try your best to recognize these souls. Ask to sit down with them and offer to help heal their disease, lest they contaminate others. One final note: you must release any and all resentment associated with the holders of vast fortunes. You must not be jealous, and you are not to fear wealth. For if you do, you will lose all you have gained. You will take your million dollars and squander it at the gambling hall. Do you understand? Clean the slate once again. This is good and sound advice for all undertakings.

What can we do about people breaking into our databases and stealing our information?

Do you have something terribly sacred that needs protecting? You would answer indignantly, *"Of course! Our records of birth and assigned employment numbers and licenses and such."* If you could only see this from our vantage point. There is nothing of essential value within the thousands upon thousands of bits of data in your computerized records. The only thing of value is your connection to Source, to the Almighty One. And that can never be taken from you.

Your possessions and records are something to keep you occupied and distracted. Some of the stealing occurs to give you still more to occupy your minds. You are probably quite surprised to hear that. But think about it for a moment. Recall a time when you were blissfully happy. Not a thing in the world could bring you down. You were soaring through the Heavens, so high you could touch the sky. Your brother calls to tell you that your fence collapsed and you remark, *"That is simply wonderful. I will fix it someday."* And that is that.

Now take this idea and expand it. Some of you have already done this. Advanced souls endure tremendous loss and bounce back with hardly a scratch. You who have accomplished this must speak to your brothers and sisters to give them hope. You must lead the way for those who cannot yet envision their own strength. We will give you this suggestion for a middle ground in which to work…

Do your research and take steps to protect what needs no protection just to satisfy the fearful ego while you are learning to embrace the greater Truth. Know that it is your perception that serves as the all-important rudder of your vessel. Allow your intuition to guide you. If you must lock the doors in your neighborhood, then do so, but without fear or dread. Are your actions driven by memories of past hurt? Do you aim to keep an enemy at bay? Remember that it is not what you do but the intention behind your actions that matters most.

Finally, if you do lose something or it is stolen by a soul in fear, simply go about replacing it and hold no resentment toward this individual. Speak to him in your mind if you feel it necessary and say all. State what you expect from him and do not forget to hear his side. Do these things and you will be free of the nagging fear of loss for all time.

What happens with deceased loved ones? Are they happy? Do they want us to know anything?

The word, *deceased* must be clarified. Your loved ones are still with you. They have gone nowhere. Just their forms have disappeared. So you must learn to communicate in a different way. They have much to say; tune in. Be still and you will begin to hear without sound... without the eardrum, but with the Mind.

Remember that the joy and connection you felt was not dependent upon their form. You laughed and shared your smiles and your hearts. You are still connected and can share all those same things. You must learn to do this without merely seeing with your optic nerve. Have you ever sat with a friend or newborn baby and gazed into his eyes, without speaking a word? Of course you have. Did you doubt his love just because he could not speak? You have the answer.

So refer to this example when your ego tries to shoot down the idea of non-verbal communication and loving relationships with dear souls who possess no form. They are just as precious to you today, are they not? They feel the same connection to you, though you are in form. So make an effort to maintain the relationship.

You need not ask if these souls are happy. Would you not be blissful once the heavy body and all its ills were laid to rest, freeing you to float about effortlessly? You have heard of those humans who have glimpsed Heaven... seen the other side just for a moment. Do they appear happy? Yes, they certainly are as they recall their visit – smiles come sweeping across their faces. They long for another glimpse of such a beautiful place.

We will tell you what they want for you, as it is always the same. They want for your joy and peace of mind, Dear Ones. When you are sad, they are sad for your unhappy state. And when you are joyful, they celebrate your joy along with you. They want nothing more than to see you healthy and vibrant, blissful... enjoying the fruits of your efforts, realizing your dreams whatever they may be. This is what we wish for you also.

Your Father in Heaven wants nothing more for His Beloved Son. So live your lives to the fullest. Take chances and be bold. Go out on a limb for a good cause. Give of yourself and share what you can with your brothers in need. Cast aside doubt and fear, and forge ahead to create the world you dream of... the one you call Heaven. Create it where you live, and create it now.

Can you tell us about climate change?

Your planet is a living being just like you. She goes through moods and cycles. There are places in her that are unhealed just as there are in you. She has strengths and weaknesses, and things she is working on to correct. Her lessons are not the same as yours but she is part of your classroom. She is affected by your actions. Climate is a clearing of debris and a result of seasonal changes, which relate to growth spurts and resting, building and breaking down. There have been major climate changes since the dawn of time.

You have surmised that your recent defiling of earth's atmosphere has brought about the most recent dip or rise in temperatures. Granted, there are some erratic geo-cosmic occurrences that your scientists are scrambling to explain. We would also agree that your defilement of earth's skies is an abomination and must be corrected. But we tell you truly… her cycles are not based on or determined by your use of gas-driven automobile or power plants. The more important question is, what can you do to correct any human-caused imbalances? Now that is a better direction and focus.

First, we suggest that you cease the endless monitoring, testing, recording, and sample taking. It serves no real purpose except to line pockets and give momentary but false self esteem… actually, *ego* esteem. Instead, switch your focus and efforts to the animals that have begun to perish. Spend the funds and help to provide homes for them as their current land and water homes vanish. Identify the causes of their dwindling resources. If you are honest, you will see that your species is responsible for these shortages and the drop in their individual numbers.

Can you create alternative homes for them? Of course you can. Do you realize the interconnectedness of all God's creatures? So the question that might follow is, if you need every animal and bird, insect, grass, and tundra, what happens if and when they perish like your ancestors, the dinosaurs? We tell you that all species are still with you. They simply [trans] morph into a distant relative or remain in the earth's soil, dormant until their time to reappear. Now for the tricky part. You must work to save every animal and insect and grass from extinction as you bear in mind their eminent extinction. That again is an example of the duality of your world of form.

Intention is what is truly important, Dear Children. It is more vital than what actually happens on this plane or any other. It is what lies in your heart and what you value and nurture… that is what determines the direction evolution will take.

If you carelessly allow earth's inhabitants to die off one by one, you will lock yourselves into many more lifetimes of pain and loss, and personal suffering. It is not an easy concept. We ask that you trust us. The best gauge for knowing if an act makes sense is simply how you feel as a result of following through with it. So we invite you to test any of these theories for yourself. Just remember to distinguish between mere ego gratification and true, authentic joy that is your natural state.

Do we have a soul mate? Can you explain monogamy?

You have many soul mates… many choices to help you with your studies. And your choices keep changing, Dear Ones. The reason being, you are continually changing. So your choice – the one that attracts you – is the very same mate that would best fit the need for assistance with the lesson at hand. Do you understand? If he does not attract you, then he is not the right one, and not the best specimen for the present undertaking. We will elaborate.

If you have issues with deserving… believing that you are not worthy, then you will be attracted to a mate who will give you the best opportunity to speak up and exhibit greater self love by finding your voice when he criticizes you. If he is physically hurtful and abusive, then you will be given perhaps many chances to claim your worthiness by blocking the next punch… ducking when he attempts the next blow to the head. Do you see?

Now let us discuss monogamy. The male of the human species is not designed for monogamy. He is less apt to remain interested after the act of procreation. The long-term conditioning and near brainwashing has impact on behavior. But building a life together has its own rewards. As we have explained before, there is great purpose in the stretching and pushing beyond the limits with respect to the human experience.

In nature, it is more common to see males in one group and females in another. But again, we have witnessed much pairing for life and find it impressive and something to be modeled after. The vast majority of you see merit in remaining together for the lifetime. We do not believe it has merit, however, when the union is no longer based in love. If you remain together for less admiral reasons, we cannot condone such a decision. On the contrary, working diligently to keep your relationship strong and filled to the brim with joy is to be commended.

We repeat, do not remain in the contract for reasons lacking value. Do not stay for monetary gain or out of a sense of duty or guilt. If you think your mate will be hurt by your leaving, know your choice to stay will inflict greater pain for your partner. She may be too weak to walk away. You do no favors for this mate because you cannot feign requited love when it no longer exists. Seeing your face every day reminds her of what you no longer feel and she is apt to turn it inward, blaming herself for a failed marriage.

Marriage is not often in sync with what was intended by union... to serve Love. It is a union for purposes of learning, not a legally bound imprisonment intended to keep humans together to create stability and generate funds for a greater tax base. Do you understand how these once wholesome ideas have become bastardized and tainted? You must work to untangle them to find the pearl of wisdom.

This is what we suggest. When you are unsure if it is time to part, have a meeting with your partner. If tensions are high, speak in the mind first. Follow the same procedure we have set forth many times before. Once you have spoken and said your piece, ask him to speak. Do you wish separation and require validation? Then speak to your heart first and ask the question there. Make clear what you are feeling. Are you bored? Are you afraid to give yourself fully to this mate? Perhaps you are trying to solve the problem of self love. Thinking you are undeserving, you hoist this heavy load upon her shoulders, expecting her to repair the wounded self.

Of course it cannot be solved in this way and therefore you are bound to come to an end. You then walk away and start over until you feel revealed and vulnerable again, at which point you will again leave the union, citing irreconcilable differences. Do you see the patterns we have laid out for you to recognize yourself in? Take your time with this. Make no change in haste. You will know when it is time to move on.

Why does Spirit remain silent when children are starving?

We remind you Dear Ones, you signed up for the class… all of you. We cannot interfere with what has been decided. There is purpose and great importance to this particular lesson. Whether you are a starving child or the mother who watches in horror or the stout spectator thousands of miles away. It is still your lesson and you are impacted by it. Even when you seem not to care, we see the silent tears you cry in the night. For this is your child and your mother or wife, and it is also you.

You cannot escape the pain it causes the Sonship to watch as an innocent child perishes when a morsel of food could have saved him. All the while you feast on far more than you could possibly eat and discard enough food to feed thousands of children every day.

Do not think for one moment that your Father in Heaven does not see and does not care. Again, this is your lesson, and you must complete it to move to the next level of study. Do not forget that you live forever. The child who collapses and whose body is left for the vultures to devour is at peace… freed from the emaciated body in the clutches of hunger. He is free to play and sing and dance while he contemplates his next adventure.

So be light of heart as you also take action to correct the injustice. Can you write a check? Of course you can. So what is holding you back? Participate in this life, Dear Children. You can skip no class, so why not complete it now? The child you save – the life you spare – is your own.

Does it hurt Americans when we hire foreign workers?

This question is addressing two separate issues, so the answer will be twofold. Let us address greed, which is the primary reason to engage in the practice. We have spoken about it at great length. It is toxic to the body… a disease that will corrode and corrupt every cell and every system in the body belonging to the Son of God. So weed it out without haste.

Begin by reconnecting with your families and friends, neighbors, and townspeople. Hold local gatherings and invite all to come. Then you will see the faces of those who have been displaced by greed. These are the people who are now lacking employment due to the practice of sending the work to a lesser-developed country to increase the prized bottom line. Invite stockholders to these meetings. We recommend that stockholders, and especially those who sit on the board – the decision makers – be present at these local gatherings to witness and participate.

Try this experiment. Give just one job to someone who has lost their livelihood and see how their face lights up with joy. The return of self-confidence is of great importance to the health and well being of this soul and your townspeople.

The second issue is quite easy to address. Of course it is wise and healthy to give work to those in need, regardless of where in the world they reside. If you can help improve their lives by doing so, then by all means do it. But do no such thing at the cost of hurting someone else. Here is a demonstration to help you…

You prepare a feast. You have a house filled with hungry people and you also have hungry neighbors. Who do you feed first? The answer is yourself and your family and then your neighbors. Because your responsibility is to yourself and then to your family and then you are to share your surplus with your neighbors and anyone else who comes along. Do you see?

You do not love the neighbor any less. The idea is that you do what you can for those closest to you, as that is necessary to keep a home. Use this approach for national matters in just the same way. You are to care for your countrymen and then the welfare of people throughout the world. It is not favoritism... it is order, and there is a difference. Those who stand at the front of the line are helped first. If you feed your neighbors while your family starves, there will be much turmoil in your household. So keep order and give all you can when you have more than you need.

Some lawmakers propose law that is misleading. What can be done about that?

Ah yes... deceit runs rampant among your brothers, Dear Ones. It is not a pretty sight. We believe it has nearly run its course, and that is a blessing. Here is what we suggest: speak to these lawmakers in the mind and state what you will no longer tolerate and what you expect of them. Then speak to them at organized rallies and write letters. Collect signatures and hold meetings to brainstorm ideas but keep it peaceful or you lower yourself to their level.

Remember that they are elected officials, working for you. If you cannot convince them to amend their ways and you cannot find decent replacements, then you must lead the way by paving this road yourself. Take a leadership position. It is something you have always wanted to do and the time is ripe. So sign up, Dear Leaders. The world needs your honesty, wisdom, and strength. You will never look back in regret, and you will not miss your uninspired current employment.

Should abortion be legal?

The legalities are not the issue, though you believe that is the right question and focus. The real issue is, why invite a soul to join you and then change your mind? The canceling of a joining together as a family is a statement and testament to the undeserving mentality of human beings. Bringing a soul child into your life and into the world of form is a special event and deserves respect. But like so many other things you humans have adulterated, you engage in the act of copulation without thought... without a solid foundation of love and intention to create union and family.

So in a sense you are inviting something and then shutting the door on it. It is akin to inviting someone to dinner and when they arrive, there is no table set and nothing on the stove.

The act of lovemaking is not intended for entertainment, to stave off boredom, or to repair a wounded sense of self. To the sound and whole, balanced human, coupling is an expression of love. Mated souls confirm their union and a desire to create greater closeness and a stronger bond. It is not about satisfying a temporary flair up of hormones. That, by the way, is not a normal consequence of the body in a balanced state, though you would never know it. Your body form has been bastardized for quite some time.

We can offer this. Take some time off from the frenzied daily routine. Travel to a pristine place and leave your electronic gadgets behind. Take in the clean air and bask in the sun. Speak not a word and drink only from a natural spring. After a day or two, you will begin to settle down. You will undoubtedly be thrown off by the unexpected calm and peace that come over you.

This is your innate, God-given tranquility and emotional well-being, stripped of the customary caking and gunk that create chaos of mind and body. Remove yourself from polluted water and defiled air that the sun must filter through, your diets of dead food, and your electronics, which include the hyperactive deluge of images... the barrage of gun-toting characters and expressionless robots.

You must find your way back, Dear Ones. The time is now. You have taken the charade as far as you can, and you feel no joy as a result. Return to the Self and you will find an ease and peace that you have only dreamed of. If you engage in a sacred coupling as a result of joyful connection and close companionship, there will be no need to cancel what you have created.

Your fear comes from a sense of obligation, both emotional and financial. But if you are participating in a balanced loving partnership, the news would be happy and no other kind would be possible. Only those half participating would consider aborting what they have made together.

Know that you are eternal beings. The canceling of an incarnation, as decided by all three souls, merely undoes what was planned. It is impossible for just one or two to decide to abort. The decision was made unanimously. That is on a *soul* level. The children riding along in the backseat will see it differently. Do you understand? So take each step deliberately, for the guilt that you hold from such a canceling will likely haunt you for lifetimes to come.

What should we do about the threat of nuclear war?

This inquiry is related to your question about terrorism. Do not spend time in dread, Dear Ones. You have nothing to be afraid of under any circumstances as long as you do just one thing. There is only one requirement to keep yourselves out of danger. You need no alarms, no guards, and no electric fencing. That one requirement is to love. And your love must extend to *all* your brothers, not just those you deem worthy. Ah, that is the catch, as you say.

You must love all things. Embrace every event, every moment, strangers, friends, and family alike... your enemies included. Can you do this? Of course you can, but *will* you? That is the real question. We have spoken of this before. You must lay down your weapon and refuse to reengage it even if your enemy tricks you, pretending to lay down his and then attacking you with it. And how do you handle this obvious and underhanded maneuver?

You look him in the eye with the heart of compassion and brotherly love. This is how you protect yourselves from attack. You love your brother with all of your heart. Now how does that translate and break down into a specific action? We will explain.

You must withdraw your weapons. We realize most of you are unwilling to do this and are in support of your military arming itself to the teeth. You believe in showing your might for all the world to see – the bulldog snarling and growling, and ready to bite. So here is a solution you can live with…

Speak to one of the nations that you currently see as a threat. Invite them into your mind and speak of your fear. Express your concerns and state what you would like. Do you wish a truce and ceasefire? One must be pure of heart in a quest for peace. Now allow this nation-soul to express its concerns and desires for your relationship. Continue to extend your heart to these warring countries, and as you do, you will realize your own participation in warring. Cast no stone, Dear Children, for you are not innocent.

Once you have said all and they have replied, allow love to wash away all sin. Do not delve into the past. Do you truly desire peaceful resolution? You must wipe the slate clean if you want to be free of worry and retaliation. Do this simple exercise with all nations you feel are a threat. It will take several nights and perhaps many weeks. If you have followed our direction, you will be sending a blanket of peace across the oceans.

Do not underestimate what you are creating. It has tremendous power to heal. You will begin to see minor and then greater changes coming in various forms from all corners of the globe. What is left – the physical machinery which you think has power to destroy – will actually have no effect at all, not unlike a grenade which fails to detonate. Without hate to fuel it, even a nuclear bomb is harmless.

Do you understand this important message? It needs to be understood as it applies to a multitude of areas of thought. The only thing to be feared is your own hate… your desire to harm the self, for that is what needs correction. It is the frightening bomb that needs to be disarmed at once. Spend time in the silence and ask for help. We are here, Dear Children. We will guide you every step of the way.

Why do men and women see things so differently?

You created this disparity. Your Father had no hand in it, for you are the creator of your life. It was your intention to create a challenge for yourselves, and that is exactly what you have. The effort required to come to an understanding is substantial, indeed. But what a grand reward you enjoy at the success of it. How many things can you say that about?

Males of the species choose the highest peaks to traverse and so you choose a woman just as treacherous to conquer. Beaming with pride, you bring home your well-deserved trophy. But you also show off your scars with delight. Females are likely to do the same. *"He is this and he is also that, but I made it work. What a fine specimen I am!"* So you see it would be no fun at all if there were only peace and tranquility among the sexes.

You would have nothing to talk about at your dinner tables. It is almost as delicious as inviting a charismatic, foreign diplomat to tea. You smile and listen intently as he tells his colorful stories, and understand not a word. Then you bid each other farewell and you cannot give any details of your time together because the conversation was inconstruable. You can always choose to converse with your comrades and sometimes you do. But it is far more interesting to admire the bejeweled trophy with indecipherable wording engraved upon it rather than fraternize with your colleagues, discussing the boring within the predictable.

Now we suggest the next time you find yourself complaining about the frustration you feel over your many attempts to comprehend a simple conversation with your dear soul mate, remember what we have said here and give thanks for your Holy relationship with your twin self. It is quite extraordinary, wouldn't you agree?

<u>*Is there something to be learned from Hurricane Katrina?*</u>

Yes, Dear Ones… there is. An important lesson stands in its wake. Do you know what Katrina is? The surge of disharmony and turmoil submerged, pushed deep down into the tissues of the soul that is you, the earth, and all her inhabitants. It could not be stopped, erupting and laying waste to everything in its path. It was your pain and your hate. You are both the perpetrator and the victim… the criminal and the innocent recipient. You could not stand one more minute of inequity: the mistreatment of a suppressed and oppressed class of beings, well deserving of all God's gifts. It is you.

We understand the concept is difficult. From your vantage point, it seems that there is one side against another, one doer of harm, and the innocent ones receiving the blows. Your hearts go out to them, as they should. But we remind you… all contracts are mutual. These brave and courageous souls volunteered to endure tremendous pain and anguish so that you, Dear Humans on the upside, may learn what it feels like to kick a brother when he is down.

You are seeing many demonstrations all over your planet and repeatedly in your neck of the woods. The cries can be heard as they circle the planet and echo through the canyons. The Ancient Ones who live in the mountains weep along with you. Do not doubt it.

This knowledge should give you strength to persevere and carry on, for you are nearly at the summit. The [social] classes will not last, for they cannot stand in the face of truth. They were created as protection for the upper crust of society, who worked diligently to keep the lowly down because they feared them. It was their only weapon. But the poor of possession would not remain silent for long. It must be remembered that stomping on a brother while he is down is detrimental to the soul. It continues to haunt and make miserable the doer of such a deed.

So the storm in the heart became a storm of great power in a small state. Many eager students in an overcrowded classroom… they all came to witness and participate in the event. But the studies have come to a standstill. The lesson books are collecting dust as most of the students have fled. It is important that the course reach completion without delay. If you live in the region, begin at once to repair the damage.

You may start simply by bringing some of these fine beings into your mind and speaking honestly to them. You may say that you fear what will happen if they come to power, owning companies and running banks and diners… and you are afraid of what will happen if you must work under one of these souls whom you have wronged. You fear his retaliation. Or you fear a man of color will marry your daughter and you will be faced with harsh words from friends or neighbors.

Explain to these souls how you were raised, and how you were told that people from their tribe would do harm or were not worthy of the same things you of the light-skinned tribe were entitled to. Be honest, Dear Ones. For that is how to solve the problem.

Now as always, allow him to respond. There is nothing to fear. You are in the safety of your mind, and ego cannot enter. Look this brother in the eyes and see the sadness and also the understanding and quiet tolerance. We remind you… do not allow guilt to enter your sacred meeting. You are here to find solutions, not hijack or derail your progress.

Know that you are a continuation of earlier generations, born of ignorance. You are to take what they formulated, make corrections, and build upon that. So if you possess some degree of wealth, send a check and bless your brothers in need. And if you are a brother in need, speak up and speak out. Start the conversation in your mind. Conduct a meeting and make your demands. Do not hold back, lest you allow anger to produce disease in the body.

Now state what you require of those who have done harm. Does your home lie in waste as the well-to-do enjoy their remodeled mansions made of marble and garnished in the finest fabrics money can buy? Speak of this and the shame that keeps you up at night as you toss and turn only to awaken to the nightmare once again. Be still then, and ask your brother to speak. Do not skip this part, Dear Ones.

Wait in the silence. If you cannot yet take this step, ask for strength to begin the forgiveness.

We tell you truly, there is power in the mind meeting. With pure intent – one to heal and bring light to a darkened place – miracles will come forth. The finishing of the lesson is required, as we have stated before. Delay no longer. If all you do is send healing light and love to this wound, that will be enough. Spend just five minutes stating your intention to fill the gaping hole with Golden Light. Will you do this?

Those students of more advanced studies, hold a meeting in the mind and invite the heads of state. Bring those individuals who have the power to correct the situation… to clean up the mess and rebuild. Complete the process by allowing no judgment. Be respectful and voice what you need; then ask them to speak. End your meeting with a warm shaking of hands. See the contract signed. Now release any doubt. It is done.

Can you take a trip to visit the area? Your presence would be a powerful testament to the promise of change. This is what you can do and what you can learn from it. If you learn the lesson now, it will not need repeating.

Are vaccinations causing any problems?

Do you wish confirmation? Yes, they are causing a multitude of physical and emotional problems. Nerve damage runs rampant as a result of its widespread use.

When you are ready, follow the trail back to its proponents. Delve into your history. It will serve you to do some research rather than merely obey the rules set before you, born of ignorance or selfish intent. Once you have done this, bless your lost brothers, for it serves no purpose to condemn them. It is your job to solve the problem, not keep it alive through hate.

You are still convinced that germs are the culprits for so many of your ills. While that fear exists on such a large scale, you must find inert and harmless replacements for the vaccination ritual. Then you can move beyond it. Do you see? Remember to allow your brother time to accept a new idea and use no force; do not thrust it upon him.

Life is so beautiful and then there's death. How can we live 5,000 years and can you show us the other side?

Dear One, you may live as long as you like. As you know, humans lived for a thousand years, and then they decided to shorten the life to change things up. It is a common practice in your world of form and duality. Humans are prone to desire change and also dread change in the same breath. That is a prime example of the fractured self. So your shared dream with your brethren at this point in time is to leave the body at the one hundred mark or thereabouts. But it is changing.

You ask the question because many of you have decided that a century is much too short. You would rather live several lifetimes back to back. Hence, you are returning to a lifespan of a thousand years. Would you truly wish to live 5,000 years? You are eternal, and that cannot be measured. We believe you are more concerned about dying than living. Now that is something to address.

Your fear of death is not valid. You dread that inevitable moment when you take your last breath, but you cannot see the forest for the trees. By the time you are in your final days of the current incarnation, you will have evaluated all that you have accomplished, as you have done many times during the life. You will ask yourself, *"Have I done all I can here? What shall I choose next?"* Satisfied with the completion of your studies, you are ready for spring break.

Your lives are a continuum… a continuation of the prior school year and curriculum. You choose instructors and classes, study partners, and so on. You consider all you have learned and enjoy a sense of accomplishment while you rest and share the recent life's experiences with your brothers in the afterlife. Then you return to pick up where you left off.

So your questions are really more about the fear of death, which is common for humans but also nonsensical, as there is no death. You live forever, so practice your faith. Have there not been a thousand opportunities to do so? Take one of them and try believing when you cannot see what lies ahead. Do this repeatedly until you build your faith like a muscle, to the degree that it is dependable; strong and reliable when you need it.

We can describe the other side, as you say. Imagine the most beautiful day in the most gorgeous place on earth. Everything you see is glistening with golden rays of sunshine… every tree and mountain and lake. Every living thing is enjoying this pristine and beautiful place with scents so lovely, the nostrils long for more. Every color of the rainbow fills every speck of even the tiniest creature or plant or drop of dew. It is the most Heavenly place you have ever seen or dreamt of. There is peace here. It is the other side of the coin. What you have taken and turned ugly, Heaven is its complete opposite.

What you should know is that it is also your creation. Heaven and the illusion [life on earth] are actually the same place. But for an instant, you have dressed the setting with the dark mood of the moment and written the dark script that is your current experience. One is real and the other is its shadow. Do you see? The illusion is simply a place of scholastic endeavors. Once you no longer need it, the place you are so afraid to leave will mean absolutely nothing to you. For how could you prefer it over the Heaven we have just described?

We know this concept is not an easy one. But you are here in this moment of sacred clarity, reading our words of hope and encouragement. It is a time for courage, so let fear fall away as you move toward greater joy. When you miss your home, come to the sea and speak to her, for she knows your heart and all your secrets. Nature is your connection to Heaven, just as we are your connection to the Father.

So live your life to the fullest, Dear Ones. Do for others and give your life meaning by participating fully in the restoration and resurrection of the Holy Son of God… for he is you!

Can you please explain free will?

Yes. Free will is a precise concept with a specific definition. But you have taken the idea and expanded it far beyond its meaning and scope. You have spread its parameters and turned it into something it is not. Free will simply means you are free to take your time with the coursework… postpone a class if you wish, switch out instructors, drop a classmate, and so on. Do you see there is much you can do within the presets of free will?

Now we will tell you what free will is not. Free will is not foregoing the curriculum. It is not dropping out of school never to return. Free will also is not skirting your duties nor is it planting one seed and growing something entirely different. Here is an example…

You plant rutabaga, and free will says you may choose not to water your seeds. So the ground may turn dusty and the seeds lie dormant until you choose to return to your garden. But free will does not mean you plant rutabaga and spinach pops up in its place. That is not free will, Dear Children. That is fantasy.

If you do not wish to study with a particular instructor, you are free to select another. You are also free to move about the classroom until you find a study partner of your liking. [i.e., you can delay a lesson on codependency by choosing a mate who doesn't challenge you. You'll take a break from your studies with an enabling type; then choose a different partner at some point to continue the lesson.] Trust that the design of your world and all you see is divinely orchestrated… perfect, right down to the smallest detail. One day, you will see it for yourself.

Will the bees survive?

Your hard working friends and fellow earth inhabitants are much farther along the path than you. These special beings are watching over all you do. You are a young species… in your infancy. They are your professors and guardians. At the same time, they have families and are susceptible to emotional outcries just as any other species. You have brought them great harm with your modern agricultural practices and quest for greater production. Their families have suffered tremendous pain.

Everyday in which they leave their hive home to forage, the bees risk their lives. Some never return. It is a fifty-fifty gamble these days. You have lost half of the bees on your planet, Dear Ones. Is there nothing to convince you how serious this is for your survival? There is only so much you can do to produce crops without their help. The plants you are growing using alternative means or avoiding sun crops altogether are depleted [of nutrients]. The sun and natural pollination are both needed for proper nutritive value in your food supply.

But you have not been paying attention. This is just another problem you have heaped onto the great pile of which you spend little if any time contemplating. You say, *"Other species have died… so what are a few more?"* It is settled. You cannot be bothered. You have always survived every disaster and that is all the reasoning you believe you need. But Dear Ones, you have not the insight, nor the wisdom that comes with experience to see where this most alarming trend is leading.

You have plenty of evidence. You need not one more study to see what is happening. Most often, research serves to delay. You could have it solved if you truly wished. But instead you look busy, shuffling the papers on the desk and pretending to be out of breath, lifting the heavy volumes around the office. All the while you are looking for ways to continue current methods. Some of you appear to be solving the problem. You designed new packaging with cheerful caricatures and slogans that say, *"I care about bees."* But you fool no one.

What can you do for them, you ask? Set aside a square mile in every small town, and several in larger cities where the pollinators can live unharmed and undisturbed. Turn off your gadgets. Do nothing to harm them. Refrain from collecting their honey, as that is their sustenance and food for the winter. Have you not looked on the store shelves and seen your many alternatives? Of course you have. As in so many other areas of your lives, you have not seen the point in making a change. It is simply not important to you. Your slumber is deep, children.

You have tuned us out and learned to sleep through the sound of a bulldozer and the wrecking ball. That is the point at which we are, Dear Ones. We will spell this out for those who must have the details so they can record the findings and report back to their committee heads.

The honeybees are vanishing quickly from your planet and they will not likely return. They may change their minds but it would require that you make an about-face, and it must be done quickly. These precious creatures are being poisoned. They fly through airborne chemicals that drift and spread with the wind from the fields and lawns you spray. You must discontinue this harmful practice at once.

The towers, which carry the signals for your electronics are also a problem. They must be housed rather than free to emit signals in and through the air. You have not looked into other options, as you did not see the value in it. Engineers, inventors, and visionaries already have the answer. So seek them out and work together to save your brother insects. It can be done, and it would give you a great sense of accomplishment to succeed in this endeavor.

We will give you a leg up. Look at previous technology, which you discarded… your first attempt at portable [car] telephones. It is a decent compromise. You need not have a gadget, which fits in the pocket, as it is a health hazard to place such electronic vibration against the body. The compromise would be a blessing to humans. If you would but cease the electronic games for a mere 3 days allowing for the loosening of their hold, you would rediscover the joys of group participation, preferring it over solitary games. Meanwhile, your insect friends are waiting to see what you will do next. Will you care enough to ensure their survival?

If you miss this opportunity, your lives will be quite different. It is only a matter of time. You lack foresight. If you do not know which chemicals do the greatest harm, here is the only test you will need. Take one week off from stimulants and pollutants so that you can reengage your sense of smell. If you will not stop smoking, drinking, and eating tantalizing concoctions [processed foods] for even seven days, then enlist the help of those individuals who are living clean and ask them to conduct the research.

Now fill your automobile with five large packages of the chemical-laden product you wish to test. Open the packages so you can detect their odor. Now roll the windows up and park your vehicle in the sun. Sit for fifteen minutes breathing the air inside the car. If you can breathe easily, then by all means use these gardening products or cleaners. But if you begin to choke as we suspect you will, then discard these lethal toxic compounds and mixtures where they can do no harm.

Of course that is impossible. They will evaporate in the sun and come raining down and flow to the seas. You will breathe and eat and drink these very same chemicals, so you are in danger too, Dear Ones. You merely have a higher tolerance than the tiny sensitive pollinators with their large eyes wide open. We have taken much time here to warn you of their eminent disappearance from your planet. So heed our warning and refuse to participate in the poisoning of your planet at once. We cannot say anything more. It is time to trust.

Is being gay okay or is it wrong?

This is another place for you to lay judgment. Remember that any area of strong response [overreaction] has meaning. For there is a past hurt [trauma] that needs tending to. [Regarding judgment of gays] Let us recall our discussion regarding wounded souls repeating the lesson from lifetime to lifetime to express repressed emotions. The alcoholic parent who raised you is now your spouse, or perhaps the alcoholic is you. This is how you humans address and heal your past pain, through the act of repeating… setting the stage in precisely the same fashion and inviting the players to reprise their roles and continue the story.

A soul may have been male in the previous incarnation and now chooses a female body. But the lessons suit a male body, and the male personality is merely a better fit for purposes of learning. If a human is considering the idea, difficult circumstances will tip the scales. So he may flip the switch. That is the best way to describe the transformation that takes place.

Sometimes a human child leans in the direction early on. Many times the prepubescent soul is still weighing things out and is undecided. He may design the life so that equal amounts of both types of hormones are present so he can switch freely without much notice and without being obvious about his choice.

The desire for a particular body type is not truly what is being sought. It is more accurate to say there is a desire for a specific *energy* type, whether it is masculine or feminine. Do you see? We as your Guides recognize male and female energy rather than body shape or reproductive organs as a distinguishing factor. To judge a human based upon physical characteristics is meaningless.

You have made your judgments about souls who are in the middle... undecided or in need of the freedom that ambiguity offers. They do not wish to be classified, or they may wish to be conspicuous and have found a blatant form of attention-getting by looking one way and acting another [i.e., a male dressed as a female]. Do you see all the possibilities that the choice offers?

There are many reasons for the decision to be in one body and act as if they are in another body type. The option is often associated with experimentation. It can cause fear or ridicule, and it may be considered courageous. Humans are also prone to changing their minds. As you can see, the gay choice is not consistent, nor predictable even within one clearly defined group.

As far as the legality of how to regard these individuals, we make this suggestion. Treat them the same as any other soul who is searching and discovering themselves. Allow them to blossom in whatever way that best serves their soul's purpose. All God's Children are to love one another. The Golden Rule applies here and everywhere else in all situations... to do unto others, as you would have others do unto you.

If you cannot stomach contact or even the sound of the high-pitched voice coming from the male physique, then create the feminine image in your mind to match what you are accustomed to. Know that these souls are deserving of kindness and patience as they explore their world as both male and female. If your fear is just too great, then you must crack open your schoolbook and look for the appropriate chapter on self love. For you are being guided to participate in order to clear the blockage.

If you leave the lesson unattended, then you are apt to strike out in fearful rage, attacking and befalling a brother for fear you may join in their explorative activities. You may be curious and attracted to these individuals but unable to participate for fear of judgment or reasons of promise and [marriage] vow. Then engage at a safe distance in the dream state. That will alleviate the pull and false allure that is born out of attraction to the forbidden.

Know that the males of nearly every species are inclined to explore and be adventurous due to their nature and innate patterns of seeking variety and greater physical arousal. This is due to their appendage. Sensors are far more exposed. This was intentional in design. Males are fighters and conquerors, geared for competition. The appendage drives much of these traits, although some females do well at feigning the extremity in order to gain a similar mindset. Refrain from judging your brothers while in their chrysalis state. They have not yet donned their beautiful wings.

See these souls as you would any other brother who is working through his studies and that includes all of you. Do not look down on a brother because he has not yet finished a lesson. He trails you in some areas and is ahead of you in others. Do nothing to harm your brother, as this stunts your own growth. If you are in fear, speak to this brother and tell him what you are feeling. Ask him to help. Then remain still as he responds to your request. If you drop your prejudice, you will find a warm soul similar in mind with many of the same wants and concerns as you.

There is no coincidence that you attend the same school of Higher Learning. Look around you, Dear Ones. All the players in your life are chosen carefully. We remind you... there are no mistakes.

There has been a recent surge in this group. Do you know why that is? Have you watched what happens to a dam when it begins to crumble under its own weight? What happens to the water behind the wall? It rushes forward with great force as it strives to rebalance itself after a period of pent up energy. That is what you are witnessing in the homosexual community. Applaud their courage and accept their place on the bench with you. They have as much a right to it as you.

We seem to be living in times of great upheaval and fear. In what way can we be of greatest service to one another?

We are glad you asked. The answer is quite simple. Be present, Dear Ones. Focus on just one thing at a time. Drop the multi-tasking of which you are so fond. Be still. Listen to the beating of your heart and seek answers from within. That is all – just these simple points. For if you concentrate on just one task, just one problem at a time, you will clear the mind of its chatter. Be watchful to allow no other thoughts to cloud or distract.

Ask this often: *"What shall I do in this moment? How shall I approach this concern so that I may learn what is needed?"* That is how you can be of service... for you are your brother, your mother earth, and your fellow earthlings. It is all you. You have simply broken yourselves into eight billion pieces and turned on one another in your confusion. Let it go. Let the illusion disintegrate into dust. You are nearing the end of falsehoods. Those who have not prepared for the Coming [the return to God Consciousness] are holding on with all their might. That is what you are witnessing and believe is the worst of times. But truly it is the best of times.

Be grateful that it is nearly over. There is much ahead that is far greater in content, depth, and joy, worthy of the Son of God. So let this dream end. You do this by recognizing yourselves in the faces of those you meet. They are reflections of you. If you cannot see it, then that is your prayer, Dear Ones. Start there and refuse to don the ill-fitting clothing of your adolescence. Like the shedding of old skin, make way for the new. It is time. The long awaited end of separation is upon you. We are watching in eager anticipation of your eloquent and joyful transformation.

Are negative events simply our curriculum here?

We must remind you that your use of the word *negative* is a judgment. If you remember that all events are designed for your growth and highest good then all events are positive. Do you see? Let us now address your question with the understanding that *negative* in this context means *challenging*. The answer would be, yes. For the schoolwork at hand is meant to challenge and help you expand your mind to stretch your capabilities. Life is here to challenge you and that is a blessing, Dear One.

Whoever told you life was to be spent in a lounge chair? If life is lived in a healthy manner, there is balance... moments of contemplative thinking, devotion to task, and then respite. Just as you work and then play, have active hours and then retire, as the body needs recharging. It is your perception that makes the process painful or a delight. It is up to you, as we have stated before. Do you wish to see beauty and have joy, or are you determined to experience hardship and sacrifice? We have an assignment for you.

The next time you feel like something negative is in your midst, stop and seek a quiet place. Be still; breathe deeply. As you exhale, affirm that there is truth and perfection in the moment, regardless of what your ego mind is spewing. Now ask to see the situation differently. What are you missing? There is something you have misinterpreted. So spend a few minutes in the silence until you know what it is. Now you can transform it.

Give thanks for the event, as it propels you ahead of where you stood before. There is more light shining around you now. You can feel the warmth caress you as it flows through the crown of your head and throughout your body, down through the feet and circling back around to the top. You are held in a sphere of Golden Light. You must endeavor to see all events as perfect. Even if you do not yet believe it, affirm it. Be patient and it will become so. Remove the word *negative* from your vocabulary. That is the best way to see all things.

Is deep drilling a problem?

Yes, it is. You do not understand your relationship with the earth. She is not a storehouse… a place to grab and take whatever resources you deem necessary for your next project. You grow your plants and trees and when ready, you bring in machines to uproot and haul away without even an ounce of gratitude. This planet you inhabit is your mother, Dear Children. She is sacred and deserves your respect. You have disconnected from her, and that has caused you much discourse and suffering.

Your methods of drilling and excavating are not respectful. She is speaking to you. You must learn to tune in and hear what she has to say or suffer the consequences. You believe oil collection is needed to supply your vehicles and heat your homes. But there are other methods yet to be discovered. You have grown dependent and are in a rut… doing the same thing [using the same methods] over and over without love of it. Do you see how it causes you pain to lack inspiration and joy in your daily work?

We suggest you return to the ways of your ancestors by giving thanks for everything you receive, including the bounty that earth provides to you. Speak to the trees, and the rivers you dam up. Begin to reconnect with your earth sisters and brothers in all forms and your joy will return. Have you considered a job with greater value, caring for your planet? Do your research. Newer jobs are sprouting up everywhere. Seek them. You will never look back.

Can channeling – inviting Spirit into the mind – be dangerous?

We are happy to clear up the misguided teachings and perceptions. First, you must understand that inviting Spirit to speak is akin to asking your grandparents and scholarly professors to engage in conversation. You are Spirit, Dear Ones. You have merely forgotten, because the world of form is heavy and tends to cause drowsiness. We urge you to awaken from your slumber.

The act of listening and taking down information from Source is a natural act and must not be feared. But remember that misguided souls come in many different forms and the formless. Again, do not judge according to training and conditioning born out of fear. Be still and ask your Guides, appointed by God, to make the distinction for you.

It is quite easy to recognize an unbalanced soul. Can you not tell the difference between a kind and loving being, and a derelict intending harm? It is no different in the world of Spirit. There are souls who are in the midst of a lesson, which holds great importance and has tremendous impact.

They may try to enlist other souls to help them with it, not unlike the abusive husband who aims his arrows of self-hatred in his wife's direction. If she does not move out of the way, they will strike her. Hence, if you invite a wounded soul to your home, you are likely to encounter a series of what you would consider negative consequences.

Remember that you can uninvite this being if you are through with his antics. Be firm as you instruct him to leave or he will not take you seriously. There are recorded stories and tales of the remarkable and unbelievable concerning visits from the formless. But only the sensational make it in the record books. Why not focus on those events that you would consider miraculous and Divine?

Humans are inclined to be attracted like a magnet to the eerie and frightening, the gruesome and the horrific. Some individuals purposely entice lost souls to their abode. We do not recommend it. It will not be so easy to convince them to leave once they have made themselves at home.

If you do encounter one of these disadvantaged souls, speak to him in the same manner you would any other brother. Say what is in your heart and state what you wish of him, and remember to allow for his expression. Give what you can to these beings, knowing it is a gift to embrace a soul in need.

You are entitled to ask for your own space. Now you can set them free. They are learning and on their path, same as you. We end by defining a channel in this way: you are tuning in just like you would turn the dials on your radio.

What you listen to is up to you, so choose carefully, in life and in Spirit.

What are your thoughts on gun control?

If a soul has fear or hate in his heart, then he will lash out with whatever means are available to him. Making laws to deter such individuals and attempting to curb their behavior is futile. You must get to the root of the problem. If there is fear of loss and belief in happenstance, then a soul will think it necessary to defend himself, and a weapon may be enlisted as force or might.

But can you see the flaw in this reasoning? We have alluded to it repeatedly throughout this manual. You view perpetrator and victim as two separate parts [individuals] but we do not. Both believe in a world without order and fear their unpredictable brothers.

Humans want a *one size fits all* solution… a quick fix… one pill to remedy all ails. But that has led to your current system, which has offered no real solutions and no healing. Similar to the imprisoned souls, spend the time needed to find out where their pain [fear or anger] lies. What has yet to be resolved? Work with them one by one.

The task seems daunting. But if every one of you took just one hour out of your week to sit with one of these wounded brothers, your problem would be solved in no time at all. You will not consider it unless this soul is a family member. But that is where you are mistaken, Dear Ones. All God's Children are your family.

Why do people have allergies to foods, pollen, or the sun?

We are glad you asked. This is a large area to cover, but we will give you an overview. The specifics are not what is most important. The soul is attempting to make his world more comfortable by limiting himself and his choices. It is also a distraction of immense proportions as it wastes decades and even lifetimes. The humans work diligently, trying to solve the puzzle. They ask, *"What remedy should we try next?"* The physician happily dispenses more medicine and orders more tests. But none are needed.

Clarity and removal of mental debris is what is needed to clear the allergen. Let us illustrate. A soul steps out in the spring day and begins to sneeze. He retreats inside to the safety of his abode and exclaims, *"I am allergic to milkweed."* So he stays indoors all season and his symptoms disappear. Now we will shed light on this anomaly.

A lifetime ago, this soul fell in love with a beautiful young woman. They dated for a time, frolicking in the meadow near her home. The flowers were in bloom among the milkweed. A few months later, she had a miscarriage and the relationship abruptly ended. He was deeply saddened by the loss and he felt the gaping hole that was left in its aftermath. The following spring, he came out to the meadow and felt the emptiness and sense of unfairness that come from loss of a love. He sneezed once or twice and thought nothing of it.

The next time he came back to the meadow, he had a sneezing fit and never returned. The sting of losing his mate and the resulting anger and sorrow remained with him. He came into the next incarnation with its memory keenly embedded in the frontal lobe of his brain. Now a toddler in the new life, he begins to sneeze as he plays in the grass at a nearby park. His parents are unaware of the allergy's origin. So they take him to doctors and begin medicating this young soul. Do you see how it works? There is always a reason for everything that happens.

The more important thing to focus on is how to remove the obstacle [emotional wound] and clear the pattern. We have done this for you, but we will repeat it, as it is new and must be made into habit. This is done through repetition.

Here is the process. If the allergy sufferer is you or a youngster, then speak in the mind to the body just as you would a friend with whom you are not fully understanding his actions. If the sufferer is a child, do this on their behalf but make sure to invite him and do the work as a family.

First, ask your question about the symptoms. Be respectful and patient. You may say, *"I would like to enjoy this particular food but you do not seem to be agreeing with it. Do I have to avoid it entirely?"* Make sure you communicate your concerns fully and give the body options for its solution. Do not merely order it to comply.

An alcoholic might try to convince his body to tolerate his high consumption of spirits, wanting the liver to be resilient. But the body's wisdom must not be ignored. Symptoms have purpose. When the reaction is due to an emotional wound, then it should be cleared. But if the food or habit is harming the body, then the imbalance that drives the destructive behavior must be addressed first.

We will now discuss allergy to the sun. The condition is rare but is gaining some momentum. It is necessary to stop it in its tracks. Your sun is the source of your nutrients. It feeds your skin and bones, nails, hair, blood and organs. Every cell needs this vital energy source. It is quite misunderstood, so allow us to clear up the confusion.

The sun cannot damage you. The sun is a cleansing and nourishing body of fireballs and electrodes, shooting and streaming toward earth in a [way] shower. As it comes closer to your atmosphere it loses much of its power. The temperature becomes cooled enough to allow for life and still warm enough to sustain you. The idea that the sun can do damage is a fabrication. It is just another place to lay blame and keep fear in the driver's seat. So let us take this illusion of a solid structure apart, brick by brick.

For a moment set aside the test results that prove a theory of allergic reaction. You know from your scientific research on quantum physics that your world is in continual motion, ever-changing according to your belief. So it is time to take that discovery and make use of it.

If you are adversely reacting to the sun, it is time to speak to the body. Ask what it needs. Then ask your brother, the sun, to help with the lesson. Ask this: *"Can you show me how to transform my chemistry, Dear Sun, so I can enjoy your caressing rays of love as they warm my body?"* Then wait in the silence. If you cannot hear the answer, continue the exercise until you are able. You may discover that an old emotional wound stands in the way of your complete healing.

Sit quietly and ask for healing to begin the forgiveness process. It is not necessary that you know every detail of what happened to cause fear to bubble to the surface. What matters is that you heal it. Remember too that toxins lying dormant in the body tissues will push through the skin when exposed to the sun. The skin is a vast expansive exit point. Be watchful what you allow in… [unhealthy] food, water, thoughts, and images on your television screens. If they are negatively perceived, they form toxic material in the body and in time will grow disease.

Do you now understand how deep these issues lie? There are layers upon layers. It is our quest to help you find the best ways of removing error. [Speak to fair or damaged skin – let go of old programming and establish a healthy new relationship with the sun.] We remind you once again to embrace rather than curse the condition, which is in need of correction. Anger and resentment become glue in the blood, clogging the delicate arteries and nerve impulses. So be watchful of your thoughts. Hold only those you wish to cultivate and see multiply.

Why are we attracted to other people's bad news?

This is a fine question. These are the last years of the ego's reign. Do not spend time worrying about the *when* of it all. Just listen to our words without the calculations and record keeping. You are about to enter a great era… bereft of killing and pain. Many of you have already begun to see what lies ahead. It is your job to guide your brothers and sisters out of darkness. What can you point to in your lives that constitute darkness?

Whenever you ridicule or find humor in a brother who is in pain, you are diminishing the light on your planet. When you see a soul in need and you turn away, you extinguish the sacred torches that light your path. The answer here is quite simple. Stop the hurtful behavior. When you have an opportunity to help, do so. You come to these forks in the road on a daily basis, Dear Ones.

The next time you observe an unkind act, will you speak? Will you give your coin to a needy soul? Remember that you are not here to condemn or denigrate your brother. Find ways to encourage good and decent behavior without using the old tricks of guilt and coercive pressure.

If you are bothered by a publication's unkind or deceitful journalistic practices, make it known. Write a letter or speak to them in the mind. To those in charge, tell of your pain and how you wish them to behave in order to help repair what they have damaged. It is valid to correct injustice. We give you this: *In a loving way, hold people accountable.* The order of these words is important, so read it again and make sure you understand it.

So bless the brothers who engage and participate in fear-driven jobs, employed by managers who believe one must scare or shock people into purchasing their wares. It is a way of thinking that is soon to be obsolete. If you hold one of these positions, we suggest that you search your heart and memory for something more rewarding. If you see emergency personnel working diligently to pry open a mangled automobile while a brother clings to life, see no entertainment in it. Send your prayers at once. And refuse to give your money to those who peddle fear-based wares.

What can we do about our government's mounting debt?

The system is heavily problematic and deeply flawed. It is in the basic design and cannot be repaired. The structure will have to fall. Pooled monies funneling into a large holding tank, manned and monitored by those lacking character and scruples, is akin to asking the wolf to guard the sheep while the herder is away. A dozen will disappear by the time he returns. Souls who start out with good intentions become persuaded to convert to an unscrupulous mindset. There is power in numbers, Dear Ones.

If every one of you in each town attended a meeting to discuss purchases to be made – road paving projects, trash collection proposals, or schools to be built – you would have no debt whatsoever. Townsfolk would feel a sense of pride in participating in their community's projects and activities.

Each of you would happily pay your portion, knowing roads are being repaired, children are being provided with educational materials, buildings in need of repair are being renovated, and your town is made more beautiful in the process. There would be no waste, no abuse of monies, no stealing of funds to spend on wasteful things, because there would be accountability. You are far and away from this honest, hands-on method of city government spending.

What you have now is a runaway train that is about to derail. We suggest that you gain control of the engine before this happens. You must participate. Take office and speak. Make your voice heard. You have power, for you far outnumber those who have taken the helm and abused their position. Your problem is that you would rather sit in your easy chairs and watch your television sets. This is your downfall as we see it.

You are comfortable… content to have blinders on. You hear the rumble of the early tremors and pictures have begun to fall off the wall. But you merely turn up the volume to drown out the sound.

If you are ready to participate in the direction of your lives, take just five minutes and be still. Turn off every machine and take a deep breath. As you exhale, clear your thoughts and have just one intention. Ask what you can do to help. Wait until you hear something; it may be subtle. You may get an answer several days later during a casual conversation with a stranger.

You humans have thousands of problems that need fixing. Do not become overwhelmed. Just choose one area in which you can volunteer a small task. Perhaps you will write a letter, or attend a town council meeting. Pray for courage, Dear Ones… for yourselves and for those who mind the money.

Speak to one of them in your mind and state what you wish of him. Again, do not attack. Be respectful and honest. You would likely do the same thing had you been in the position. You condemn your brother, but you are all capable of greed and hurtful acts. So have compassion and never give up on your brother.

What causes Alzheimer's?

We will give you information to help comfort those who watch the slow deterioration of a loved one. First, you must know that our hearts are with you. It is painful to watch you go through and also difficult for the one who suffers, because he does not remember the agreement. It is not how it appears. The disease is temporary because you are eternal, so take heart. Whatever you witness is like a bad dream. It can do no harm because you are merely dreaming. Do you see?

We suggest that you become still as we have previously instructed. Speak to your dearest one in the silence. Remind him of your love, loyalty, and eternal devotion. You are reminding both of you of the perfection of life by engaging in this simple act of faith. Now tell him he is free to leave the body and the life when and as he sees fit. If you are having problems with this step, practice acceptance until you are at peace with the situation.

Now let us zoom in on the specifics. Why would a soul choose an illness that is predicated upon a lack of awareness and memory ability? It is intentional, but be sensitive to those who suffer as not to reveal truth until your brother is ready. A condition in which one becomes helpless to the point of needing constant care, has its rewards. Has this human been quite independent for the past eighty years? There is a desire for nurturing that he may have postponed until the end of his life. The hardest of lessons are often put off until that time.

We suggest that you spend as much time as you can muster to develop your skills in non-verbal communication. If this classmate chose you, it is likely due to some carryover from a previous lesson and lifetime. So embrace it. Enjoy your time together and do not spend precious time asking *why*. When he feels frustrated or frightened, hold your beloved's hand and show your acceptance in the eyes, without words, for none are needed.

Know that you have been chosen for a reason, and it is an honor. If you have things to say to this brother, then say them in the silence. Give thanks for your Holy Union and trust that you will be together long after the laying down of the form. It is written by the Hand of God and will remain so for all eternity.

Why do you use mostly masculine pronouns?

This question relates to the dual nature of your world and the illusion that there are many when there is just one: One Son…one Child of God, just as you see eight billion reflections of the One. So asking which of the shadows are feminine and which are masculine is not easy to answer. Here is our attempt. In this context and for purposes of clarity, you are all masculine. But again, there is truly no masculine nor feminine. It is a tool for the mind to allow for better comprehension. It is also a distinction to separate one physical type from another as they relate to procreation.

There are some differences, absolutely, which we have made clear in previous discussions. The roles of each as they pertain to Holy Union are important. But these are merely the outer dressing, which has no real meaning. If procreation is no longer needed, then there need not be a masculine nor feminine form. Do you see?

The second was created to allow for multiplication… to populate your planet and make real the classroom experience. As you leave the world of form, the distinctions between one sex and the other fall away. Your species will morph into a combination of the two. We are not ready to say more as the unfolding will reveal all when it is time.

For purposes of this manual and all other teaching guides, know that together, you are the essence of God's Love… His one Begotten Son in totality. You must cease the narrow focus, which gives any importance to one sex over another. It would be as absurd as favoring one plumbing pipe over another based on the shape of its conjoining part. We imagine plumbers do not think male tubing is superior to its female counterpart. Your species has shifted many times from patriarchy to matriarchy and back again, like the ebb and flow of the tides.

We use the masculine throughout the manual because it is more accurate than referring to two types of children, although we occasionally use both terms. You are all brilliant points of light emanating from the spectrum – reflections of the One Son in all his glory. You are like individual droplets of ocean, and together, you are the sea. This analogy should serve you well. Remember it when you feel separate or powerless. When you join together, you are more powerful than you could ever be apart.

We give you this to help those who feel inferior or superior: you are all equally important to the tapestry, regardless of intelligence, possessions, skin color, body type, age, spoken tongue, and all other attributes. None of these things matter in the least, except that what you have chosen serves the curriculum for the present lifetime.

If your brother is struggling to grow in the shade of the towering oak that is you, nudge him gently so he will thrive in the warmth of the sun's rays. And if you are the sapling striving to establish your own plot of earth, claim it with all the power of your young lungs. You must know that it is yours and no one can take it from you. Others will then step aside and honor your chosen space. You are worthy, Dear Ones. Never forget it.

Computers are a big part of our lives. Is that a problem?

Are you ready to hear? Then it is time to look up from your distracting gadgets. You think you have made great strides with your technological advances. And you have, but where is it leading you? Do you see the cliff with the 1,000-foot drop just ahead? This is an important question, indeed. If you wish to learn the lesson with greater ease, then catch this wildfire early before it burns down the forest.

Can you see how your time spent on these machines and devices has affected your relationships? The hours waste away and when you emerge from the fog, you must reacquaint yourselves with the living. It is time to take stock of the situation.

You can solve this without returning to the horse and buggy, as technology is not the problem. The disease that is growing is your lack of connection and your turning away from your brother in need. The one in need is you, though you do not see it. For you cannot be happy while your brother suffers. How is he suffering, you ask? Let us now look at how technology has altered your workplace.

Do you remember not long ago when a human being connected your calls? The operator was a colorful, charming character, playful and inquisitive… a lover of people and conversation. She was an invaluable source of information.

Many women were employed in this field. Then your modern telephone systems replaced her and she was cast aside, tossed out like refuse with not even a thank you. The receptionist was the next head on the chopping block. Then followed countless workers whose jobs were replaced by machines. And the trend is growing, and picking up momentum.

Those who stand to gain from these decisions are pleased as punch. *"Ah, we have doubled our profits, gentlemen! Let us give ourselves a hand and a raise."* Now you know what goes on behind the boardroom doors. But what of the workers who fall one by one like dominoes? This explains the rapid decline of your middle class, and the numbers continue to fall. This also relates to your question about the rich getting richer. We are revisiting the subject of greed. It is a tumor in the body of man and a large part of this discussion.

Computers are not the enemy. The problem is a growing disregard for your brothers… a general selfishness and lack of connectedness. A computer brought in to help with the smooth operation of a vehicle, firing pistons and making combustible calculations for safer travel, put no one out of work. But a computerized machine that replaces an assembly line worker… that is where you must consider your choices and how they will affect your community.

We urge you to make no decision in haste while dollar signs dance before your eyes. Think carefully before you act. Hold a forum to allow your brothers to speak. Do this even though you do not see the danger in your current way of doing things. The one who loses her job today is of no concern, for you did not know her. But tomorrow, it is your mother, then your brother, and then it is you. We do not wish you to stop all use of computers. What we ask is that you consider the consequences of your actions, in all areas.

Why can't people just be nice to each other?

It is entirely possible and we wish that for you. But you have chosen to learn through resistance rather than joy. This is the classroom, Dear Ones. It is a place to work and complete your lessons. You prefer to romp on the playground all day long. You have avoided your studies, making them into a chore. And now you are truant.

An example is the weightlifter who cries, "*Why do I have to lift these heavy weights?*" Because that is how you build muscle… by pushing beyond your capacity and the limits you set for yourself. Being nice to each other is seen as a luxury available only at respite. Once a lesson is complete, you are relieved of some of the heavy burden and so you search your pocket change and say, *"I can afford a smile today."*

But kindness is not something you need to work up or create. It is innate. Those who hide their joy are in fear, and you have made a habit of it. Do you see? The angry and smile-less faces are deep in coursework and often amidst finals – pressured and without sleep.

You must also understand that there are helpers on your planet. Those who possess a lightness of Spirit are here to help lift God's Children. Next time you are out among throngs of people, be aware of the many faces you see approaching and passing, and you will recognize these souls. Nod or smile in their direction to give thanks for their mission and assistance. You can join them. How can you do this, you ask? Decide to give just half of your thoughts to your imagined dire needs and problems.

Think more the way you do on vacation. You are light and joyful and engage in conversations with strangers with ease. You do not worry about your mortgage, your child's grades, or the neighbor you despise. You are kind… generous with your heart and your wallet. Now do that same thing when you return home, and you will solve a grand portion of the world's crises.

We tell you this: lessons need not be painful. What makes them so is your resistance, as we have stated before. If you would but allow the rain to fall upon your heads, you will see it is not what you feared. Once the dark clouds begin to form, invite the rain and embrace the lesson, knowing the sun will reappear, even brighter than before.

For you more advanced pupils, we suggest this: begin to see when your mood shifts and catch it there. Stop it in its tracks and transform it by extending kindness to even the worst of clerks. Generously tip the unhappy food server. For she is suffering, is she not? If she is open for a moment of clarity, take her hand and look her in the eyes with a gentle smile and wish her well.

You Children of God have countless opportunities to help your brother in need. Money is not a requirement. A kind gesture goes a long way. Lifting the Spirit is a precious gift of which you are all capable. So make the effort. Embrace your studies knowing they will lead you out of darkness. There is no need for a world of strife. Drop the illusion of struggle this very minute. Declare that you can and will learn in an environment of joy!

<u>*What is the best way to call on you for help?*</u>

As we have stated throughout this guidebook, begin by being still. Ensure there are no distractions and make clear your need. Then allow the answer to come as you wait in the silence. If you cannot hear it, repeat the exercise until you can. But remember what we have said previously… there are souls who wish only to continue as before, leaving their desire as merely that. So the problem is not as serious as they claim. If that is the case, then allow yourself time to reach a point of urgency in your request for assistance. Then you will be more motivated.

Remember that each individual is unique. There is no clock ticking away with an alarm about to blare. The day will come when you are ready, and genuine is your intention. You will refuse to take *no* for an answer, and that is when you will hear us.

Know that it is akin to learning a new language, though you have known it since time began. You have been away from your homeland for so long, you have forgotten. So learn to recognize the subtle nuances and inflections in tone. We may sound more like your thoughts. You might say, *"That is just me. I must be imagining it, just filling in words."*

Do you not see that we are there in your thoughts? That is where we live. We speak to you through your intuition. So learn to tune out everything else. We are always here for you. It is our purpose and our joy to help you find your way Home.

What is the most important thing you want to tell us?

Love one another, Dear Ones. That is the most important thing you can do, and *all* you need do. You have your lengthy *To Do* lists and countless errands to run. You are always rushing with hardly a minute to spare. Obligations loom over you as you read this book. But if you would for just one day let time be unimportant, you would discover peace. Leave the timekeepers in the drawer. Glance at not one clock for an entire day. Will you agree to it? We sense you desire a reward of some kind. So do that – attach a reward. Then follow through with this assignment.

For one day, be free of time. Take a day off and fully engage your playful side. Enjoy a rollick in the grass or lie on a sandy beach and allow a wave to surprise you as she calls for you to join her. Do something entirely different with your day. Spend time at a park, or a center for the elderly. Sit beside a child confined to a hospital bed, or visit the animals as they peer through the bars at a shelter, waiting for one kind soul to free them. Perhaps you will take paint to a canvas as the sun begins to set.

Whatever you choose, give it your full attention. Be still and listen as your heart speaks to you. You have asked a myriad of questions but there is only one question. *Who am I?* It is more accurate to ask, *What am I?* The answer is Love.

If you would merely remember what we say here and put it into practice, the hundred or thousand questions would fade and dissipate like condensation on a windowpane. And all you would have left is love. Pure in its essence… the distillation of all you think you are and all your searching. Now let us show you how to make use of it.

If all you are is love, then ask, *"What would love do?"* In all circumstances under all conditions, without exception, love would and could do no other thing than to be itself. Will you try it? Just for one day or one hour, do only as love would. It may be harder than you think.

Give it your attention and devotion, and you will be pleasantly surprised. If you gave the exercise just one hour, try two the next time. Extend it with each effort. Find that place in you that knows all; the part of you that has the answers to every question. That is where you will find us.

Take what you have learned here and share it with your brothers and sisters in every continent across every sea. Study your materials until you know them by heart. At which point, you give life to your every spoken thought. With each inhalation, you christen each word with God's Love.

So go out into the world, Dear Ones. Make new your beliefs so the world of illusion can be transformed. That is your assignment of which you are quite capable. Do you desire a better world where peace abounds… a choir of harmonic voices singing together in unison? We know your Heart and your answer, for you are born of the sun and given life… breathed into you by your Holy Father.

You can pretend to be something else, but you are God's Beloved Children embodied in form for a moment while you explore and play. Soon it will be time to return. You have so much to share with Him. Tidy up before you do, for cleanliness is next to Godliness. Prepare for the Coming. It is almost here. You have lost no one, as you will soon discover. The Sons and Daughters of God will reunite… and you are a part of it, Dear Ones. Be glad in that knowing.

sunflower and honeybee

Epilogue

We have given you much to work with, Dear Ones. Now the ball is in your court, as you say. What will you do with the information? Will you marvel and utter exclamations of awe and then do nothing more? Or will you take action?

You have the tools to transform your life and everything you see. Like rings in the pool emanating from just one pebble, your songs of love will ring out as one resounding chorus, spreading its message of joy throughout the Kingdom.

There is no limit to what you can accomplish. Take this good advice and begin applying it to various issues in your lives. Test our theories, and take life's quizzes as they pop up. Do you recognize the ego? It is the recurring theme... the same obstacle in every story. It is the only thing standing in your way. So let it go.

Know that all you wish for is already given you. It is your inheritance. Learn to listen, and you will hear us throughout your day. That is the only map you require; the guiding light in the night. Now go forth, Dear Children, and tell the world of what you have learned. Your brothers everywhere are just like you. Your dreams are theirs. Your pain and your joy... they are also theirs. So look for commonalities and not your differences. This is the key to freedom. We leave you with these phrases to ponder:

*Every Child of God is homesick. Now you know why you often feel empty inside.

*Lift your brother to give him hope. For you cannot be truly happy while your brother suffers.

*You desired to touch and to laugh. These were the beginning points that spawned all else.

*Faith is the doorway to change. Allow a new perspective by making a place for it.

*There are no right or wrong turns, for there is perfection, even in the supposedly wrong choices. All paths lead you Home.~

The Lion and the Lamb

Take the hand of your enemy, your brother
For you know you walk this path together.
The rich man will open his heart
To the man walking along the highway
Wearing all he owns.
The classes will dissolve
And the day will come when the lion
Will lay down beside the lamb.

People ask how I came to hear angels. Eighteen years ago, a heartfelt relationship came to an end. I took it hard. One night, I prayed to repair things between us and suddenly, I felt a door open. In my mind was a scene from his childhood. I could feel the anger and fear in the room. I wanted to help so I began speaking about forgiveness and the perfection of life. My words were eloquent... like something very pure was speaking through me. Tears fell and a sense of peace came over me.

Spirit's perspective is vastly different from our own. The following examples demonstrate what's possible...

Transforming Relationships:

Several years ago, I met a man who said his marriage ruined his life. He shared some of the details. His wife was making it difficult for him to see his child. He agreed to try release work.

The session was conducted over the phone and I invited my angels. Everything was done in the mind. First, we set our intention to bring peace to the relationship. I saw a small room with a door and a bench. I told the man to invite his ex-wife. He was instructed to share everything he was feeling.

He spoke of her mistreatment of him. There was much anger and sadness. Then it was her turn. She began to speak and became filled with emotion and regret. There was a moment of understanding between them. As the session ended, he felt a heavy weight had been lifted. He had forgiven her. Soon after, his wife called, sobbing. She regretted treating him badly and agreed to let the boy live with him. He was stunned. A year later, my client met a lovely woman. They are happily married now.

Long Distance Healing:

A few years ago, a dear friend was hospitalized and not expected to live. He was in ICU, sixteen hundred miles away. I asked my angels how to help and they showed me.

I visualized placing my hands just above the injury, bringing healing to the area. They showed me inside the brain. I saw what looked like a blackened forest after a fire. There were piles of broken nerve impulses. But there was also a strong electrical current. I envisioned Healing Light, beginning at the crown, flowing down his body and out through his feet, creating a sphere. I covered him in a blanket of healing at the close of each session.

His community prayed for him. He fully recovered that year, which is nothing short of a miracle. We can always help a soul in need by sending love and light. Just come from a selfless place and ask to be guided.

<u>**Summary**</u>:

This book is our first collaboration. My Guides wrote the content. I laid my hands on my keyboard with eyes closed, typing what I heard… like taking dictation. I edited the sections, breaking them down into paragraphs and checking word definitions.

Angels are phenomenal problem-solvers. They are also very respectful. If you ask something that you aren't ready to hear or if it's just not your business, they will tell you. I really appreciate the homework they assign and their requirement that seekers must participate. They clarify so much in this book. I feel truly blessed to have the opportunity to work with these remarkable teachers.

It is my hope that this book will help you find solutions and inspire you to connect with your own Guides. Whatever your beliefs, there is a source of comfort and wisdom waiting for you. Blessings on your journey.~

Fear Not…
For the World Is But Illusion.
You Are Soon To Awaken,
and the Sons and Daughters of God
Will Laugh and Sing!

CPSIA information can be obtained
at www.ICGtesting.com
Printed in the USA
FSHW02n1740100918
51994FS